Sister Jaguar's Journey

Sister Judy Bisignano and Sandra C. Morse

Library of Congress Cataloging-in-Publications Data
Sister Judy Bisignano and Sandra C. Morse
Sister Jaguar's Journey: A Nun's Ayahuasca Awakening in the Amazon Rainforest

Cover Design: Tony Edelstein, Curious Sky Design
Cover Photo: Sophia Lyn Sims
Back Cover Photo Insert: Britta Van Vranken
ISBN 13: 978-0-9909688-1-8

See the film, *Sister Jaguar's Journey*, by these same authors.
http://www.sisterjaguarsjourney.com and www.maketaithebook.com

Designed by MyBookDesigner.com
Printed by ArtBookPrinting.com in the USA

2248837

Sister Jaguar's Journey

A Nun's Ayahuasca Awakening in the Amazon Rainforest

This book is dedicated to

all of Pachamama's children,

especially those held in her embrace

in Ecuador's Amazon Rainforest.

Pachamama is a word used by the Kichwa people living in the South American Andes. *Pachamama* means *Mother Earth, Mother of Time, or Mother of the Universe.*

Proceeds from the sale of this book will provide educational, medical and environmental assistance for the Achuar people.

In loving memory of Maria Uyunkar Taish and her two baby girls

Maria, you once held the promise of your people in your hands.
Pachamama (Mother Earth) now holds you and your baby girls in her
hands. Nothing has changed because Pachamama holds us all in her
promise for all eternity.

Acknowledgements

Thank You to our friends at The Pachamama Alliance, Inc. in San Francisco, CA. You educate and inspire individuals throughout the planet to bring about an environmentally sustainable, spiritually fulfilling and socially just human presence on this planet.

Lynne and Bill Twist

David Tucker

Tracy Apple

Lindsay Dyson

Pat Jackson

Thank you to our Achuar friends in Ecuador's Amazon Rainforest, especially in the communities of Wayusentsa, Kusutkau, Tinkais, Wachirpas, Sharamentza, Sua and Kapawi. You reach out to us in the modern world though we threaten your very existence. You issue a call for us to work with you to *change the dream of the modern world* by questioning our culture of over-consumption that drives the destruction of your rainforest and our world. We hear you and support you in this mutual endeavor.

Celestino Antík

Simón Santí Antík

Tutrik Froilan Antík

Angel Etsaa

Guído Etsaa

Sumpa Wawar Etsaa, Shaman of Wachirpas

Jiyunt (Isabel) Uyunkar Kaníras and little Natem

Kuji Uyunkar Kamiras

Remígio Santí Panky

Alfedo Palora

Antonio Shakaí

Ruben Shakaí

Rafael Uyunkar Taish, Shaman of Wayusentsa

Eduardo Tentets

Jorge Yaul Tentets

Sekunnia Tentets

Enríque Tsamarín

José Wasum

Thank you to our Kichwa friends in the Andean highlands for sharing with us a deep reverence for your culture and community while living in the modern world.

Manuel and Lora Guatemal, San Clemente Community

Don Estaban and Rosa Tamayo, their son, Jorge, and grandson, José

Maria Juana and Antonio Yamberla

Thank you to Michael, Sophie and Elliott Morse, Rayna Gellman, Kai Parmenter and Debbi Stocco for your ability, creativity and honesty while proofreading and editing our manuscript.

Thank you to our friends, the Pacha-People, who support us and our journeys to Ecuador in search of meaning for us and our world.

Veronica Galaz Antonio

Holley Allen, MD

Ellen Deck

Patricia Dolan

Michael Dooley and Joan Schweighardt

Ariane Glazer

Joel Hodroff

Julián Larrea

Michelle McDonald, MD

Graham Thompson

Sande Zeig

Thank You to our photographer friends, who contributed their magnificent photos without reservation.

Nancy Bachelier – Kino Learning Center photos

Lourdes Galaz – César Chávez Learning Community photos

Ellen Deck, Patricia Dolan, Sophia Lyn Sims – Achuar territory
  photos

Thank you to Sister Mary Anne McElmurry for supporting our environmental trips into the rainforest and our spiritual journeys into prayer. Because of you, Sister Jaguar has experienced unconditional love within religious life.

Thank you to the Morse Family: Michael, Sophie, Elliott and Oren. Because of you, we know what it means to live, forgive, appreciate and celebrate on the deepest of levels.

Table of Contents

Part Two
Pachamama's People

Part Three
Prayers from the Rainforest

Foreword

By Sandra Morse

There are times in one's life that we meet someone who demonstrates possibilities for living, for contribution, for overcoming adversity that would not have seemed possible. Meeting Sister Judy Bisignano was, and continues to be, an education in living life as a valiant engagement while responding to challenges with generosity, intellect, curiosity, humor, vulnerability and grace.

After fourteen years of vacationing in Mexico, our family had already generated many wonderful experiences: hiking, kayaking, side trips, snorkeling and much more. However, on one of our more recent vacations, Sister Judy showed us a combination of her ingenuity, great love of children, abiding lifetime interest in their access to real life educational experiences, and the reach and range of her impact on people's lives.

She found one of the former teachers from her school offering fishing expeditions right by the condominiums where we stay, and engaged his services to take a fishing expedition with mostly children aboard. She rounded up the children, paid for the trip and hobbled onto the boat herself, never being one to skip an adventure despite her constant physical ailments. In two hours, the children caught enough coveted yellowtail tuna to feed about forty people at the spontaneous, ocean-side evening feast. They stood proud, enlivened and amazed at their own accomplishments. They became the talk of our condo complex, reveling in their adventure, and receiving praise from the entire beach crowd, which kept their faces aglow for the remainder of the trip.

This is really just a small example of the way Sister Judy has approached life everywhere she has been. There are countless such stories we could tell as well as collect from the many people we encounter who have been supported or touched in some way by Sister Judy. Her recounting of such instances invariably acknowledges how wonderful *they* are, and how much *they* overcame to contribute to her school or countless service projects.

The impact that one human being can have on another is indescribable at times. It makes me wonder who we are for each other that one human being could enter our lives and have such an impact. What kind of person is willing to take vows of poverty, chastity and obedience to dedicate herself to serving those in need? What kind of person was forced to endure three years as a novice rather than the required one year, and come out ready to offer her services to the world, which her Dominican Order requires?

This book is a rare and brutally honest exposition of Sister Judy's life, flaws and misgivings included. She has never shirked responsibility for mistakes she has made, and with her life of taking big risks came the potential for such mistakes. She continues to examine her ability to forgive, to question her assumptions about people she has known, choices she has made, and even her relationship with God and Spirit.

I invite you to enjoy the journey of this courageous, compassionate and generous human being as she shares her life story alongside her reflections on her faith, her relationship with herself, and her awakened relationship and reverence for Pachamama (Mother Earth) and all indigenous people on Earth.

All My Relations,

Sandra Morse

Note: *All My Relations (Ayo Mitakuye Oyasin)* is a phrase from the Lakota language. It reflects the world view of interconnectedness with all creation. It is part of many Yankton Sioux prayers, and is found in use among the Lakota, Dakota and Nakota people. The phrase translates as "all my relatives," "we are all related," or "all my relations." It is a prayer of oneness and harmony with all forms of life: other people, animals, birds, insects, trees and plants, even rocks, rivers, mountains and valleys.

Introduction

My name is Sister Judy Bisignano. I am a seventy-three-year-old Dominican Sister. Our *motherhouse* (headquarters) was founded in 1923 in Adrian, Michigan. My strongest identity in life is as an Adrian Dominican Sister. Religious life gave me the perfect platform from which to launch my life and legacy: the opportunity to study, pray, live in community and work for justice and peace, as well as social and environmental change in the world.

I was born in Des Moines, Iowa on May 3, 1942 to a reserved, refined, strong-willed Irish mother, Catherine Dwyer, and an unreserved, unrefined, bombastic Italian father, Alphonse Bisignano. It was my fate and fortune to combine the best and worst of my parents' DNA as I assumed my inherited place within the web of life, that gigantic grid or social network of plant, animal and human existence and global interaction I call *Pachamama* (Mother Earth).

My self-perception within my family has had a profound effect on the attitudes, opinions and behaviors I developed as a child and retained as an adult. For sixty-eight years I wore a chip on my shoulder as a misidentified badge of honor. While I was angry with the self-perpetuated unfairness of my life, I was profoundly grateful for the *entitlements* I received at birth—opportunities other people work lifetimes to attain.

At an early age my parents instilled in me a deep compassion for the plight of the poor. As a young nun, I became enraged at the injustices the status quo perpetrated on the economically-poor-yet-culturally-rich subcultures!

I developed disdain for authority within family, education, government, the Catholic Church and religious life. Ironically, my anger was also the motivational force that propelled me to do good work and accomplish great things. I didn't know I was angry. I thought I was determined and tenacious, while others perceived me simply as strong-willed. To this day, my three brothers affectionately call me *bull-head!*

I acquired two master's degrees and a doctorate that would allow me to contribute to radical, alternative, educational reform for children and teens. While I always had a fondness for kids, I wanted to love them from a distance while I set them free!

I questioned educational philosophies and methodologies as I empowered children with the wisdom and skills to empower themselves. Although professional success was significant, I was plagued continuously with a profound lack of self-confidence. I incessantly chanted two mantras: "I am not good enough." Therefore, "I will never be able to do enough."

Unfortunately, I preserved and passed on the bitterness of my childhood within a lifelong story of self-rejection. I numbed my pain with hard work and intellectual pursuits while searching for false idols initiated by poor theology within religious life that mistook humiliation for humility. I built my very own *golden calf* with smoke and mirrors that reflected my biases, served my ego and gave me permission to continue the self-destructive story of my childhood, fortified by adult cynicism.

In an effort to reverse my well-established negativity, Sandra Morse, a friend and professional communications philosopher, pushed me toward remote villages in Ecuador's Amazon Jungle. While sitting and praying quietly in a hand-carved canoe tied to a tree along the Pastaza River, I had the unique experience of encountering a black jaguar stalking a large white bird. The jaguar holds a powerful position among the Achuar, one of Ecuador's original nomadic tribes. The jaguar guards the portal between our everyday and spiritual worlds, where it facilitates communication between the living and the dead. According to the Achuar, seeing the jaguar was a good omen that empowered me to experience a series of cultural, environmental and spiritual events that would transform my life. Heretofore I had been looking for God in all the wrong places. At one with the Achuar and nature, my soul's quest was fulfilled. After a lifelong search, I finally experienced contentment and peace. *Sister Jaguar's Journey* is the story of my transformational passage from self-rejection to self-acceptance; from self-forgiveness to self-love.

There are two equal authors of *Sister Jaguar's Journey*. There never would have been "A Nun's Ayahuasca Awakening in the Amazon Rainforest" without the perceptive questions, guiding conversation, unrelenting persistence and unconditional love offered by Sandra Morse. Sandra provided the skills that guided my journey from darkness to light.

For sixty-eight years, I perpetuated the myth that *self-love* was an oxymoron. Sandra Morse showed me how to sit comfortably on unknown branches of my family tree. She showed me how to retell my story with the intent to relinquish guilt, blame and revenge. When I stopped judging and began loving, I found compassion for myself and all creation.

Sandra introduced me to her Achuar friends, who shared their culture, wisdom and rituals. I found peace in remote villages in the Amazon jungle simply by following the Achuar practice of receiving and offering forgiveness and peace with my ancestors. The anger and depression of my past collided with the worry and anxiety of my future. There I was, suspended in the quiet of the present moment, forever changed.

I knew my next quest would be spiritual rather than intellectual. My next journey would be inward in service to my soul rather than outward in service to the world. There, in the stillness of the jungle, I instinctively knew that prayer and silence would guide my transformational journey.

While I can say I found reconciliation and redemption in the heart of the Amazon Rainforest, it would be more accurate to say I found serenity in the present moment. *Sister Jaguar's Journey* is the account of my passage through a narrow portal of life that shot me through the vastness of the cosmos and brought me to the center of my being.

Thank you, Sandra.

Thank you, Pachamama.

PART ONE

IT'S A JUNGLE OUT THERE

Looking for Peace in All the Wrong Places

My journey started when I visited my friend Sandra Morse for the first time.

Sandra is a communication specialist, coach, and a therapist-of-sorts. Her office looks very much now like it did back then, quaint but comfortable, with a magnificent garden weaving between it and the main house. The clucking of banyan chickens greets you as you enter the front gate. A sixty-pound desert tortoise meanders about, masquerading as a watchdog.

I reclined in one of the comfortable old sofas in Sandra's office—a rustic, Mexican hacienda. Sandra's place looks like a cross between Haight-Ashbury and the Smithsonian Institute. Over the years, that old antique couch took on the shape of my own mature posterior. In looking back, I think that aging couch has shaped me just as much as this aging nun has shaped it. I received an enormous amount of excellent advice while sitting on that couch.

Sandra asked me immediately, "What brings you here? What do you hope to achieve by coming to me?"

I responded, "I have been looking for God in all the wrong places. If I don't find her soon, I think my depression will kill me." I looked at Sandra and said honestly, "I am looking for peace."

I don't remember much of that first conversation, but in recalling that moment, I can see clearly that Sandra was asking me to confront my negative life view. She was paving the way for me to discover an alternative way of being.

She asked, "Where do you think you can find peace? Where could you go to experience the peacefulness you seek?" I would answer that question very differently today. Certainly I now feel the quest for peace is a journey within, but the blinders I had attached to my heart and soul prevented me from finding real meaning in Sandra's question. While I understood on a surface level the journey to peace was an exploration of self, I had long since decided the source of my own peace was beyond me. I was convinced it was out of my consciousness, out of my present experience—not *here,* but *there*—wherever *there* might be.

"Ireland. I think I could find peace in Ireland," I suggested dryly.

My maternal ancestors were from Ireland, which seemed as good a reason as any to suggest it. My dad's family was from Italy, but I knew if I ended up going to Italy, all I would do is eat.

I offered my sarcastic answer to what I now know was a sincere question. As I sank into the sofa and into my cynicism, I watched Sandra's reaction unfold. Being the perceptive woman she is, she saw my goal was not to get assistance; it was to prove I didn't need any. I wasn't there to improve me. I was there to disprove her. If she slipped up, I would have permission to slip out, to continue to dwell in my unhappiness. I had spent good money, only to hope both of us would fail.

Sandra calmly probed. "Can you really go to Ireland?"

I was taken aback. Her question was simple, and required a straightforward yes or no answer, not like the runaround conversations I was used to.

"Yes. I could go to Ireland."

Then she asked, "Where would you look for peace in Ireland?"

I thought to myself, *Right, I'll get her this time.* "Ireland has lots of rocks. I would look for peace under the rocks," I replied.

Sandra realized quickly that sarcasm was my diversion. I think in that first conversation she made a decision not to participate.

As she retreated, she respectfully suggested, "Arizona has lots of rocks. Stay home and save yourself the plane ticket!"

It dawned on me that I had been quick to underestimate her. Engaging in intellectual games with someone who seemed to be genuinely trying to help me would only extend and perhaps increase my pain. I sensed Sandra's insistence on only candid and honest conversation could provide a way for me to question my cynicism. I also knew surrendering to happiness would be anything but easy. I was deeply committed to my physical and mental pain. It wasn't comfortable but it was familiar, and I knew it well enough that I could navigate within its parameters. My challenge now became, could I function without it? For several months I continued to polish my skills by playing the game: *Can You Stump Your Therapist?* Every time I pushed, Sandra pulled back. Every time I retreated, she nudged forward.

One day she asked me suddenly, "Have you ever wanted to visit the Amazon Jungle? I take groups to the Amazon. Would you like to go?"

I couldn't have known that I was about to embark on the transformational journey of a lifetime. I never dreamed I would go from a desert in Arizona to a rainforest in the Amazon Jungle in search of God.

As luck would have it, I found peace by turning over my ways of thinking, rather than stones in Ireland. Though I cannot yet declare that I rest in a continuous state of peace, I can say that, through my many journeys to the Amazon, I have seen the calmness of its days, the tranquility of its nights, and the serenity of its people. It has been my privilege to witness the amity and reconciliation the Achuar people offer to outsiders, the harmony they extend to each other and the protection they offer Pachamama. The Amazon Rainforest echoes stillness and silence at intense levels, and its vibrations dispelled my sadness, awakened my consciousness and soothed my pain. As I stood in that rainforest, I knew it was sacred space. I knew I was home.

My Family

My mom was born Catherine (Katie) Dwyer in 1907 in Des Moines, Iowa. While she was proud of her Irish background, she rarely spoke about herself or her side of the family. She had one sister I know of, but I never found out if she had other siblings. My connection to her heritage was virtually non-existent. I never met my maternal grandparents, and as a result, I know very little about them, especially my grandmother. I don't know how she lived and when or how she died. I don't even know her name.

Mom was a painfully shy, withheld teenager. Throughout high school she owned a single blue dress she wore by day and washed by night. She withdrew socially in an effort to conceal her sparse financial circumstances. She earned good grades in school but, given her passive nature, she never answered questions or contributed to class discussions.

After graduating from high school my mom worked at Fanny Farmer Candy Store in downtown Des Moines. As her wardrobe increased and her personality was given the chance to blossom, several former high school jocks in Des Moines suddenly developed strong cravings for chocolate bonbons. Mom wouldn't have anything to do with them. My mom told me only one story about her home life. One was enough.

My grandfather insisted that my mom not marry in order to devote her life to him. His plan must have worked fairly well since Mom lived at home and didn't marry until she was twenty-nine years old. Refusing to accept the inevitability of her marriage, her father committed suicide on her wedding day.

I'm told Mom turned to my aunt and said, "You bury him. I'm going on my honeymoon."

I often wonder how my grandfather could bequeath such a horrible legacy to my mother. He tried to destroy her wedding day and every wedding anniversary thereafter by taking his own life. It is a credit to my mother's strength that she refused to let that happen.

My mom was the smartest person I have ever known. She was a voracious reader, which was likely the foundation for her self-sustained and constant pursuit of education. Every day she sat in her favorite living room chair in front of the window and waited for her kids to walk the block home from school. She would surround herself with newspapers, magazines, hardcover classics and bestsellers from book-of-the-month clubs. My mom, before the age of Internet and social networking, used those strewn-about books and clippings as the portal through which she acquired worldviews and global understandings.

If you had met my mom as an adult, you might have never sensed that she came from poverty as a child. I have to assume she came from poverty because of that single blue dress, as we almost never discussed her upbringing. Besides being intelligent and well read, she was elegant and stylish, even as her dress sizes increased significantly over the years. You'd almost certainly have found Emily Post's *Etiquette: Manners for a New World* in the stack of books next to my mom's most comfortable reading chair.

Mom's generosity surpassed all her other qualities. She had the time, willingness, connections and money to do whatever she desired, and she used all she had for the sake of others. From distributing well over a thousand taffy apples to neighborhood kids every Halloween, to creating the first snack shop at Mercy Hospital in Des Moines, to publicly protesting the ban on laetrile as an alternative treatment for cancer, my mother was in every sense, a generous woman. However, the way she related to me was not reflective of the grace she showed outside the family, and it would not be an exaggeration to say my mother physically beat me on a regular basis.

Despite this, she was very giving in that she granted every request I ever made of her, at least when it came to money.

"Mom, may I go to Africa?"

"Sure."

"Would you be able to carpet the school?"

"Let's get high quality carpet that will hold up over time."

"Can you pay for a couple of kids to explore the bottom of the Grand Canyon?"

"Only a couple?"

My dad would joke that he had a "mixed marriage." For Catholics, the term referred to marrying someone from outside the Catholic Church. Even if you married someone from another Christian faith, it was considered a "mixed marriage," and therefore unrecognized in the Catholic Church. It took years for me to understand the political and social implications of my father's throwaway comment. My Italian father referred to his marriage as "mixed" simply because my mom was Irish! He insinuated that my Irish Catholic mother was in a class or category quite different from him. She certainly was, although likely not in the way he thought!

My dad was born Alphonse Bisignano in 1913 in Des Moines, Iowa. He was proud of his Italian upbringing. It was the essence of his entire identity. Like my mom, my dad came from an impoverished, dysfunctional family. He had at least two sisters and two brothers, maybe more, but I only knew Uncle Chuck, Uncle Frankie and Aunt Dee. My dad was quite young when his mother died, a blow only worsened by his father abandoning him shortly thereafter. He and his siblings were ultimately raised by his grandmother, a frail old woman I remember visiting every Christmas. She and Dad would catch up in Italian while the Bisignano kids, or Biz Kids as we were called, ate warm oranges from the cobalt blue glass bowl perched on the doily in the center of her antique wooden table.

My dad was a ninth grade dropout. A street kid-turned-boxer, and then wrestler, he boxed under the name "Babe Carnera," since he was expected to succeed Primo Carnera, arguably one of the greatest Italian fighters in the history of boxing. As a young couple, my mom and dad would hop among an endless number of boxing and wrestling arenas throughout the United States. Along the way, my mom could be seen holding my oldest brother, Joe, as she watched my father's fights from their ringside seats. Mom soon realized that gymnasiums, sports arenas and smoky hotel rooms were poor substitutes for a comfortable home and lifestyle, especially when my brother Jim was born in 1938.

While it took my dad a few years to transition away from sports and into business, success came to him quickly thereafter. He was a hard-working, generous man, who walked about as if he were larger than life; qualities he carried into his next sport, the restaurant business. The atmosphere and food at Babe's Restaurant were heavily seasoned with my dad's persona and charisma. He was his own floor show. Babe's Italian-American Restaurant became a landmark in downtown Des Moines, while Babe himself became one of the town's most recognized and respected residents.

There was an enormous obstacle for restaurant and tavern owners in Des Moines, Iowa in the 1930s. Iowa was a dry state; it was illegal to sell liquor by the drink in a restaurant or tavern. Today, my dad would not be an active member in the politically motivated Tea Party, but in the 1930s, he was a staunch supporter of the socially inspired cocktail party!

In 1928, Prohibition was still the law of the land, but the majority of people, my father among them, refused to obey what they perceived as ridiculous regulations. Crime and violence increased during the 1920s as Iowa moonshiners and bootleggers created profitable businesses. Living in the Midwest, they had easy access to a key ingredient in the manufacture of alcohol: corn. Moonshiners made all varieties of whiskey, gin, wine and home-brewed beer. My dad spent time working as a bootlegger, a person involved in the transportation and sale of alcoholic beverages. Once Illinois became a "wet state," it was relatively easy for my dad to transport liquor across the Mississippi River into Dubuque and down to Des Moines. Bootleggers typically bribed police and public officials. For bootleggers like my father, it was a business expense, and for corrupt officials it was easy money.

As with marijuana today, many Americans believed that Prohibition didn't reduce crime but increased it, and didn't raise public morality but corrupted it. On December 5, 1933, the Twenty-First Amendment to the

U.S. Constitution was ratified, repealing Prohibition. The manufacture, sale, possession and transportation of alcoholic beverages was no longer illegal. Simply put, Babe Bisignano was in the right place at the right time to strike it rich, and he did.

Despite my dad having no positive male role models as a kid, he discovered one thing about being a husband and father during the Great Depression: a man works hard to provide for his family. My dad was determined to give his kids the financial security and material wealth he never had in life, and he did just that. Despite this, he didn't know, or even assume that a father should know, how to relate to his kids with any emotional depth. He was an old-school Italian and, except for providing financially, he left all aspects of child-rearing to his devoted wife. On top of the emotional distance he put between his family and himself, my dad developed a serious drinking problem, which affected all members of the family to varying degrees, and contributed to the way my siblings and I were raised.

I heard a lot of colorful stories about Babe Bisignano while I was growing up, most of which I suspect he invented or embellished, given his boisterous way of being. One of my favorites happened when my dad served two six-month sentences for illegally selling alcohol in the restaurant. I was three or four years old at the time, and every week my mother would explain that we were going to the "hospital" to visit my dad. Something about those trips always struck me as strange, and I couldn't figure out why all the "nurses" carried revolvers on their hips.

The story goes like this: a lethargic guard on duty in the visitor's room at the city jail was paying absolutely no attention to visiting children when some brazen kid came up from behind him and grabbed the gun from his holster. Apparently I flailed the loaded pistol in the air before pointing it at the "nurse" while yelling, "Stick 'em up." I had seen this maneuver successfully done many times by Hopalong Cassidy on the six inch circular screen of our black-and-white TV. As the guard raised his arms to the ceiling, several people, including my father, quickly apprehended me and wrestled the gun out of my tiny hands. I like to think that this first brush with the law was the beginning of what would become a legacy of disobedience against authority.

The Biz Kids

I grew up heavily influenced by my birth order—the social niche I filled within my family. I am the fourth of five children born between the mid 1930s and 40s. While my youngest brother, John, is the only official baby boomer, born between the end of World War II (1945) and the late 1960s, we were all profoundly influenced by that period in time.

As a kid, Joe, being the oldest, was intelligent, responsible and a conservative thinker. He helped Mom by stepping up and guiding his younger siblings. He enjoyed being responsible—being in charge. He liked the power that resulted from achievement—from "fixing things," as Joe would say. Throughout his life, Joe has been focused, capable and responsible. He too has been on a journey. Over the years, he has become warm and loving, especially toward his kids and grandkids.

When Joe was three, Jim was born. Joe firmly retained his position as "the thinker" while Jim established his identity as "the feeler." I believe Joe grew in generosity and confidence, while Jim cultivated gratitude and cooperation. Jim is a natural peacemaker, and as such he hates conflict. Even as a child, he established himself as a sensitive, creative musician and artist, without the competitive streak his older brother had.

When Jim was two, Mary Kay was born. Being the firstborn girl, she seemed to have more freedom in defining her place in our family than I.

She was free to establish any niche she desired. Like her brothers, Mary Kay proved to be immensely creative and artistic. She was a good student but she struggled to achieve academic success, as her reserved nature prevented her from actively participating in class. Like my mother, she was quiet, graceful and wholesomely beautiful. Mary Kay was also a tremendous athlete, which became all the more apparent as she grew into her wiry adolescent frame.

I was born fourteen months after Mary Kay. All my life I suspected Mom resented getting pregnant with me when Mary Kay was only five months old. I was the accident waiting to happen. I recall feeling constantly inadequate, frustrated and vulnerable. Spending much of my childhood steeped in anger, I struggled to define my place within the hierarchy of my family.

My younger brother John was born four years after me. John was born with a very pronounced club foot, and I think this condition may have added to Mom's vigilance and protectiveness towards him. As the youngest, John had no one to follow behind him, but several ahead of him setting the pace. In his early years, John desired to be cared for by all of us, though as an adult John strove to individuate himself. Without question, John was Mom's favorite. Because of this, I believe John was the least supported by my dad.

One of my more distinct childhood memories is of washing the dishes for seven people every night. Whoever misbehaved during the day had to wash the dishes that night and, needless to say, I was the perpetual family dishwasher. My mom kept a running log inside the door of the cupboard that held the glassware. I remember the day I left for the convent, I had one hundred and thirty-eight more dish-washing days to work off. My mom said to me, "The only reason you are joining the convent is to get out of washing the dishes." She was close. One reason for joining the convent was to get out of that house.

I was sent to bed before dark on a regular basis for breaking the family rules. I fell asleep listening to my siblings and friends play "kick the can" in the street in front of our house until the streetlights came on. It was during one of those lonely nights that I began my near-lifelong mantra: "I am miserable. Please God, let me die tonight." It was some time before I developed a second identity outside the parameters of my family and outside that self-deprecating mindset. In the world around me, I came to be perceived as intelligent, creative, generous, intense and funny. It was only after I left home I realized I could rally this persona into a force for good.

Without question, the Biz Kids grew up in a verbally toxic, abusive home, despite all we were given. My brothers will be shocked to read my assessment of our childhood, as I am not sure they were fully aware of my darker feelings, or how those feelings, and my subsequent behavior, influenced how I was treated. I had always looked up to them and so for a long time I tried to show only the brighter sides of myself. Joe and Jim were my heroes. As young kids, they were responsible and self-sufficient. Growing up, they knew how to make the family look good, at least on the outside. They were good students, athletes and class presidents. However, as my heroes grew older, I remember them becoming more rigid, controlling and judgmental—especially toward me.

Perhaps I was too close in age to make a clear assessment, but I saw Mary Kay as the lost child. She escaped by being invisible. She had a profound stutter that my mom insisted could be cured by repeating a sentence until it was articulated with crispness. Always reticent, she would read books of fantasy to withdraw from reality, and retreat socially to avoid being hurt. She could have dated, but she didn't; largely, I suspect, because she had a difficult time expressing her feelings to outsiders. I think that she, like I, was terrified of intimacy.

All four of my siblings and I achieved success on the outside. But as we did, the family secret, my dad's drinking, decomposed us from the inside. I think his substance abuse made him incapable of connecting with us on the basis of love or compassion. As his drinking worsened, the distance between my father and the rest of my family grew more and more pronounced.

As I got older, feeling more and more like the scapegoat of the family, I believe I became the most honest as well. I openly expressed and acted out the tension and anger the other family members seemed to ignore. I received recognition within the family the only way I knew how, by being negative and disruptive. I felt tremendous shame for the place I came to occupy within my family. My childhood shame was only compounded by the avalanche of guilt perpetrated by growing up in the Catholic Church in the 1940s and 1950s. I received deeply toxic messages delivered in the name of God, and I had a hard time swallowing the Church's persecutory morality. I didn't buy it then and I certainly don't buy it now. However, it took years for me to unshoulder the idea that I was responsible for or shaped by whatever Adam and Eve did in that Garden. After a lifetime of grappling with ideologies I knew in my heart to be poisonous, I am still mending the wounds I both caused and suffered because of my family's religious beliefs.

There was one thing the Biz Kids had in common above all else: we were exceptional athletes. After Dad, Mary Kay and I were the best athletes in the family. When it came to sports, the girls took after the competitive nature of our father. Like him, we took winning almost too seriously.

Mary Kay and I developed different athletic skills supported by our body types. We were both tall, but she was lean and I was "husky." Mary Kay's body was chiseled for speed and finesse, so naturally swimming and track and field became her strongest sports. To this day, her records stand unbeaten in high jump, broad jump, and the 100-yard dash in our grade school and high school.

Mary Kay and I made playing softball more boring than it usually is. I played pitcher and she was the catcher, and anytime we played we made sure everyone in the infield and outfield stood around doing nothing. If the batter connected with the ball, it rarely got past the pitcher's mound, and together we were able to throw out most runners at first base. Mary Kay was a great hitter and an even more exceptional runner. She could round second base and be headed for third before the outfielders ever touched the ball. She had more inside-the-park home runs than anyone else on the team.

What I lacked in speed, I made up for in strength and accuracy. At the end of grade school, I had a three-year batting average of .818, which far surpassed the stats of my heroes. Ty Cobb, the greatest hitter of all time, had a lifetime BA of .366 and Babe Ruth ended his career at .342. Growing up, my batting ability became one of my few sources of self-confidence. I got on-base 40 percent of the time at bat. Ty Cobb got on-base 20 percent of the time. While this may not seem like much, it instilled in me great pride and joy because I knew my efforts and abilities pleased my parents. They were proud of me, which is all I ever really wanted. Mom and Dad never missed a game, but they also never missed a violin or dance recital or parent-teacher conference.

⊗◎

Despite my skill at softball, I enjoyed basketball far more. My extra weight did not seem to slow me down, and I could play any position and score from almost anywhere on the court. There was no three-point shot when I played high school basketball. If there had been I would have owned it, along with the lay-up and fade-away jump shot.

I have often been asked if I ever considered a career in professional sports, specifically softball or basketball. I graduated from high school in 1960. The Title IX Education Amendments did not exist until 1972. Title IX stated that, on the basis of sex, no U.S. citizen could be excluded from participation in education programs receiving federal financial assistance. While Title IX is best known for its impact on women's high school and collegiate athletics, the original statute made no explicit mention of women or sports. In answering that question, the best response I can think of is that I was born into an era and a family that wouldn't have been able to support me pursuing athletics seriously.

The Biz Kids learned early on that excellence, on a variety of levels, was both revered and expected. We did whatever it took to be successful. I remember one classic story that reveals a lot about my parents' desire to provide everything for their kids, while also cautioning us that gratitude and generosity were requirements of a privileged childhood. It was early Christmas morning and the five Biz Kids were opening up our presents. I don't know exactly how many packages and piles of wrapping paper and ribbons filled the living room that morning, but it reminded me of the final holiday rush at a Macy's Department Store. Each of us got clothes, books, games, toys and major items like bikes, ice skates, sleds, toboggans, etc. We were all delighted, except for the hard-working provider of the family. In the face of what he felt was extravagant overindulgence, my dad decided to turn the gala event into yet another serious learning opportunity for Mom's "spoiled rich kids." He ranted and raved about his poor childhood, reminding us that at that very moment, all over the world, countless children were having Christmas without a hot breakfast, presents or new toys. Apparently, in spite of their misery, all of the freezing little children, especially the orphans of the world, were happy because they had warmth in their hearts. Before Dad had the chance to finish, John, the youngest of us, stuck his head above the mountain of tissue paper and Styrofoam and yelled:

"Mom, do we have to hear this story again? We heard it on Thanksgiving."

My father, seeing an opportunity to make good on his righteous tirade, took it one step further. "Okay you kids, pack everything into Mom's Cadillac. We are going to take all this stuff to the Christ Child Home."

We were stunned. One of my older siblings asked, "Can we at least keep the new underwear? That's really a fake present."

Then it was my turn. "I thought orphans were happy with just the warmth in their hearts!"

Mom and Dad fought over the degree of punishment their "privileged" kids deserved for their insubordination. Needless to say, she lost the argument and subsequently boycotted the trip to the orphanage. When we arrived at the Christ Child Home, my dad explained the situation to the nuns. They gathered all the kids in front of the Christmas tree, and sure enough, presents for the five of us allowed twenty-five of them to each get a couple of gifts for themselves, while the whole group shared the bikes, ice skates, sleds and toboggans. As I watched the hearts of the orphans swell with joy and thankfulness, the nun exclaimed, "There really is a Santa Claus!" to which I added begrudgingly, "Yeah. But he didn't come to our house!"

To this day, every time I drive past the Christ Child Home, now offices for the Diocese of Des Moines, both pangs of resentment and gratitude fill my soul for having learned a hard lesson at a very young age: giving hurts if you let it.

The Initial Source of My Sadness

There were specific situations and events in my life that made me what I am but also prevented me from becoming all I had hoped to be. The first was a recurring incident that lasted throughout my childhood and early teens.

My secret began when I was four and continued until I was sixteen years old. For some unknown reason, my mother chose me—the fourth of her five children—to abuse physically and verbally on a regular basis.

My father kept his belts inside the door of the linen closet near my bedroom. Mom would either choose the belt or tell me to pick one, thus giving the appearance that I had some participatory power in what took place. I picked belts according to the softness of the leather or the shape and size of the buckle. One day I chose a bright green, flimsy belt with a two-inch cross-stitch that read: "God Bless the Irish!" When Mom saw the belt, she went ballistic. It was years before I realized she interpreted my simple choice of belt as a cultural slam against her Irish roots.

I would undress and position myself across the bed facedown. I braced myself for the stinging blows while vowing not to cry. Unfortunately, this common parental practice was accepted or at least tolerated by society throughout the 1940s and 1950s. I didn't know why it started and I didn't know how to stop it. The more she hit me, the more I retaliated with anger and resentment toward her and my siblings. I started to feel like I was participating in and even adding to this vicious power struggle, though my mom had all the power. Supposedly my bad attitude was Mom's justification for the beatings. Unquestionably, I had a bad attitude, one that only got worse as the beatings continued.

It didn't take long for me to disconnect from my mom as a way of coping with the beatings. I resented her, my dad, and my siblings for allowing this family ritual to continue. I escaped into my dark place as Mom withdrew into hers. As the beatings continued, I grew angrier—hating her, hating them, hating me, hating life as my negative feelings started to permeate every aspect of my thinking. I believed the only way out was to die. As a child, I spent a lot of time fantasizing that death was the only honorable way out of life.

Her abuse towards me continued throughout my adolescence. Rather than being disheartened, it began to embolden me. With each incident I grew more irate with my mother and more distant from my family. One day I simply refused to take her abuse any longer. As she chose the belt, I grabbed the loose end and wrapped it around my hand. I pulled her toward me and screamed, "It's over, Mom. Starting today, you will NEVER hit me again." I felt sorry for her. I looked into her eyes and saw her fear and pain for the first time. I couldn't tell if she was afraid of me or afraid of who and what she had become in treating me the way she had. She never hit me again. It was years before we ever spoke about it.

It wasn't until my sister, Mary Kay, died of Hodgkin's disease at the age of 23 that my mom and I began to acknowledge the pain that separated us. Mary Kay's death pushed my mom and me together as forcefully as we were once torn apart. As we buried my sister, my mom stood at her grave fighting advanced breast cancer. I stood next to her having recently beaten thyroid cancer. Mary Kay's death was our wake-up call. It was the motivation Mom and I needed to forgive and embrace each other with unconditional love.

For the next twenty years, Mom and I had a special bond quite different from the relationship she had with my brothers. Their loving relationship with Mom grew steadily from childhood, while the love between my mom and I grew eventually from adult forgiveness. I firmly believe that for the last twenty years of her life, my mom loved me every bit as much as my three brothers. This was an enormous departure from the way I understood my mother as a child.

Unfortunately, I was never able to foster a similarly loving and intimate relationship with my father as an adult. I recall my dad as being unwilling or unable to contribute to his family in a way that extended beyond his wallet. It is my understanding that Dad declared emotional bankruptcy before any of his kids were ever born, perhaps even before he married my mother. I don't know why, but my sister and I were somewhat exempt from Dad's anger and unpleasantness. The boys, however, were pummeled constantly with verbal abuse, especially John, who was closest to Mom. Dad favored me, perhaps because he knew I was out of favor with Mom and the rest of the family. Many years after Mom died, the family fighting stopped because Dad could no longer remember what the fighting was about. I suppose even senility has its benefits.

Ironically, my mom was the first member of the family to extend her hand in reconciliation towards me. As an adult, she said to me repeatedly: "I'm sorry, Judy. Please forgive me."

My mom and I were able to heal our relationship because we owned the pain we caused each other, then asked and received mutual forgiveness. I firmly believe that dysfunction infected my mom's family tree. Someone, somewhere caused her tremendous pain and she passed it on from one generation to the next. When Mary Kay died my mother and I realized it was time for us to heal our heritage of conflict.

Dysfunction is not self-correcting. It will not simply dissipate on its own. Throughout my childhood, I took on portions of the unresolved conflict I believe my parents inherited from their ancestors. I was influenced largely by my nationality, ethnicity, religion, economic status and place within my family—all characteristics I see now were centuries in the making.

While I realized I had inherited some portion of my mom's pain, I unknowingly passed it on to others. I was naive to think refraining from marriage and motherhood would end the cycle of violence that seemed to permeate my life. While I did not genetically pass on my anger to the next generation, I dealt it out emotionally to those with whom I became closest, every child I ever taught. A lifetime passed before I had the wisdom and grace to ask for and receive forgiveness for my genetic predisposition—my inherited, self-perpetuated dysfunction.

My Secret Refuge

As a child, there were only a few places that offered me refuge. St. Augustine School was located just five houses away from ours. The convent was a huge white mansion that stood at the top of the hill. The actual school was located just behind the convent, and if I wasn't home I was there at the school, spending time with the nuns. I tried to make sure I was never home, as I only really felt at ease at St. Augustine's. It was there, with the Adrian Dominican Sisters, that I found sanctuary. Their words brought me kindness, and their smiles brought me affirmation and hope. Their thanks made me want to assist them more, so I did. I spent all my time helping the nuns, eager for a smile or a thank you, hoping to be someone special in their eyes. They didn't know about the beatings. I never told them. I wanted them to like me, and I thought if I told them I would run the risk of them hating me too. I assumed I had done something to deserve the family struggles I had inherited, so I kept them secret, pretending life was fine, all the while wishing I were dead.

Just behind the school was a ravine that led to the lagoon in Greenwood Park. I knew it wasn't a real lagoon, but that was what everybody called it, and I wasn't sure what a real lagoon looked like. I just knew I could hide in the trees and tall grasses and walk endlessly around my own personal lake, which was only a giant fishpond. I found the sights, sounds and smells of that hidden place irresistible. The lagoon became my refuge, my secret hiding spot. I would curl up in the tall grass and fall asleep with the assurance that no would sneak up from behind with a belt. At a very early age, I replaced my own mother with Mother Nature, who held me tenderly in her embrace. I trusted her. I loved her. I wanted her to love me back, but I wasn't sure she did. The only assurance I had was reiterated continuously from my status within my family, which told me I didn't belong.

Looking back, it was the nuns and that special place in nature that saved my childhood. They accepted me; they encouraged me; they brought me peace. The nuns and nature offered me shelter from the pain of a brutal upbringing. When I was with the nuns or in the woods, I was safe. I enjoyed life. I belonged someplace. But eventually, I would always have to go home.

After graduating from high school in 1960, I made what felt like the only reasonable transition to adulthood: I entered the convent. I wanted to be like those Adrian Dominican nuns in whom I had seen a love for life, each other, and perhaps even me. They were intelligent and courageous, and I decided I wanted to be one of them. Joining the convent gave me an honorable way out of marriage and family life—where I instinctively knew neither joy nor peace resided. I was convinced that if I became a nun, I would not repeat the mistakes of my mother. I would never be caught in the trap of pretending to love someone. I would never have kids and abuse them, or so I thought.

Religious life provided me the platform to live in a community with women I admired who furthered justice and peace in the world. I lacked the maturity to know I could not erase my history of child abuse by refraining from having children. Unfortunately, I took my accumulated rage and carried it forward. For the better part of my adult life, I injected my anger into every personal and professional relationship and event. I rationalized my own pain by maintaining that verbal abuse was really not all that vicious. While I clubbed people with my words, I never physically hurt anyone, and so in my mind I was never *really* guilty of abuse.

Becoming Dominican

1960 was the perfect year for me to graduate from high school because it allowed me to grow to womanhood in what I believe was the most profound and powerful decade in human history. As a young nun, I eagerly embraced the sociopolitical turmoil of the 1960s as I transitioned into adulthood.

Unable to deny the demand for greater human rights and individual freedom, the United States broke free from the norms and social constraints of the 1940s and 1950s. By 1960, television brought images of war, poverty, racism and nuclear threat on a global level into the living rooms of nearly every American family, mine included. Although those years can only truly be appreciated as transformational in hindsight, I watched the 1960s and 1970s give rise to a number of domestic and global forces that increased the social consciousness of the planet. The radical and subversive anti-war movement and the Civil Rights Movement continue to call me towards a more just and peaceful world as strongly today as they did when they were happening, which is a testament to how powerfully they changed my way of thinking.

There exist many different groups of religious women, called orders and congregations. My older sister, Mary Kay, joined the Sisters of Charity of the Blessed Virgin Mary (referred to as BVMs), in Dubuque, Iowa a year before I entered the convent. As a *postulant* or candidate, I requested membership into the Dominican Order. The Dominican Sisters were founded in

1206 by St. Dominic Guzman in France for the purpose of preaching against heresies that threatened the Catholic Church in the Middle Ages. Over the course of history, however, the purpose or mission of the Dominican Order has evolved into one of serving the global good. Today, Adrian Dominicans still live simply in community as they did at the inception of the Order. We now stand with the whole Earth community, not just Catholics, as we challenge local and global domination, exploitation and greed that privilege some and disenfranchise others.

While the terms "nun" and "sister" are used interchangeably, they are quite distinct. Nuns are women who live simple, prayerful lives as contemplatives within cloisters where they rarely speak and have little or no contact with the outside world. Sisters are women who live in community for the purpose of prayer, study and service. Sisters live actively among the people they serve, generally the poor, and therefore the politically powerless. Strictly speaking, I am a Dominican Sister, not a nun. Since our headquarters, or motherhouse, is located in Adrian, Michigan, about eighty miles southwest of Detroit, I am referred to as an Adrian Dominican.

When I entered the Adrian Dominican Sisters, I was unaware of their strong position on social justice. Their core commitment to stand in solidarity with the poor resonated with my personal convictions and values. I think most nuns would describe their decision to enter religious life as a "call from God." Since I never heard God's voice or experienced His or Her presence, mine was more of a "lucky stumble" than a "divine call" into religious life. It was years before I realized and embraced the prophetic relevance of this match between the Adrian Dominican Sisters and myself. I do not think joining any other Order or Congregation would have allowed me to arrive at where I am today. The Adrian Dominicans lead the reformation within religious life in the 1960s and 1970s. I was ready for the political and religious changes we embraced.

In my formative years as a postulant and novice within the Adrian Dominican Congregation, I was intrigued and motivated by our stand on social justice: to seek truth, make peace, and revere life so all of Earth's people might know freedom, equality and full personhood. I have observed our position evolve to include eco-justice over the past thirty years. Simply stated, social justice refers to our response to injustices against the poor by curbing the effects of poverty and racism locally and globally. Eco-justice refers to our response to injustices against the poor living within the constraints of their environment, which include air and water pollution, soil loss and climate change. I have always been fascinated by Earth's ability to rejuvenate itself. Knowing the Dominican Order has come to recognize the great environmental challenges of our time gives me great pride.

Of particular concern to me is the growing deforestation and oil production along South America's Amazon River basin, which has opened the rainforest to colonization and industrialization, often with frightening results. Such growth raises alarms about the extinction of species, the loss of life-saving medicinal plants, the irreversible damage to the delicate balance of Earth's climate control system and the tragic disappearance of indigenous cultures. Today, Adrian Dominican Sisters confront modern day heresies, including the politics of institutions that disenfranchise the poor and threaten the environment the poor call home.

The Postulate

In August of 1960, one hundred and twenty-two young women, myself included, joined the Adrian Dominicans as postulants. We were the largest group to ever enter our Congregation. It took six months before we were received as novices and wore the white habit characteristic of Dominican priests and nuns. The initial six month postulate is followed by a one year novitiate, followed by five years of temporary profession. After six and a half years my group took perpetual or final vows of poverty, chastity and obedience within religious life. Final vows gave a sister tenure—a permanent place to belong.

I wasn't in the convent eight hours before my privileged childhood collided with my desire to seek a more austere but happier way of living. At home, maids and cooks exempted me from completing common household chores, except for the punishment of dish duty. The first instruction we were given was, "Go to the laundry and get your towels for the week." I did exactly as instructed and returned with fourteen towels.

The Postulant Mistress asked, "Are those towels for everyone in your dormitory?"

I replied, "No. These are my towels for the week—one every morning and one every night." She explained that nuns get one towel for the week.

I thought to myself, *how gross!* But I replied, "Well, I guess I just got towels for everyone in the dormitory!"

As a candidate, or postulant, I sought entrance into the Dominican Order. It didn't take long before I saw clearly it was a cold, unsociable environment. However, since I had been immersed in antagonism and criticism throughout my childhood, the oppression and condemnation within the convent seemed normal to me. I felt quite at home. I understood this was a trial period where I could decide if I wanted to stay and the nuns could decide if they wanted me gone. This tug-of-war lacked equity or balance, and seemed to be anything but a "grace period." Certain postulants were publicly singled out, rebuffed and deliberately humiliated. This hazing seemed contrived and disingenuous to me, as if the hardships of religious life were being exaggerated to test the sincerity of our intentions and the reality of our vocations.

I felt bad for the postulants being singled out for public humiliation and verbal mistreatment, and I knew instinctively it was my place to stand in solidarity with them. I thought first about standing up for them the way I stood up for myself years earlier: grabbing the abusive situation by the belt, pulling it toward me, and shouting, *It's over, you will NEVER treat these women like this again.* I knew I would be kicked out if I protested publicly, so I went into survival mode, watching and waiting in silence.

I soon concluded that certain postulants were singled out because those in authority had determined them to be the strongest and most forthright. I wanted to take their place. After all, I had been singled out as the strong one within my family, and I could handle the absurd components of religious life like I handled the ridiculous aspects of family life.

I devised a solution to my moral dilemma and put it into action. I went to the Postulant Mistress, knelt down, folded my hands in prayer, bowed my head and said, "Sister, I have come to ask for a favor." I guess no one had ever come to ask a favor because she suddenly quit reading the mail and turned her head sharply toward me.

"I want to take the place of one of the postulants on your list!"

She responded quickly with, "What list?"

"The list of postulants who are strong, the ones who are singled out to take unfounded abuse," I replied.

She probed further, "Why do you want to replace certain Sisters on this list I am unaware of?"

I mustered my courage and said, "I don't think they are comfortable with your yelling. I've been yelled at all my life. I can take it."

She turned back to her stack of mail and told me to return to my duties. We never discussed the topic again. However, upon concluding her daily rampage against the other postulants, our eyes often locked. She knew I disagreed with her tactics, yet I had no power to hold her accountable for the system of abuse she disguised as appropriate.

As postulants, we wore simple black outfits consisting of a long sleeved blouse and a skirt covered by an apron and a veil. Though I can't prove it, I think we stole the style from the Amish women in Amana, Iowa! We kept silence all day except for one hour of recreation, or as close to recreation as was allowed, before evening prayer. One night during recreation, the Postulant Mistress designated four of us to wash, dry and iron one hundred and twenty-two veils before evening prayer. With less than forty-five minutes to spare, we gathered the veils and headed quickly for the wash tubs in the basement. I should mention here that as postulants, we were not allowed to eat between meals. Furthermore, we were never allowed to indulge in soft drinks. However, I had developed a strong craving for Coca-Cola. As we headed for the basement, I grabbed a six-pack of Coke and a handful of homemade cookies from Sister Doloretta's kitchen. Sister Doloretta cooked for the priests, and always had the best stockpile of food. There, in the bowels of the basement, my three buddies and I soaked the veils as we stuffed ourselves with caffeine and sugar. Needless to say, the time passed quickly.

Our Postulant Mistress, a large stern woman, came down the stairs and into the basement. I whispered, "Put it in the water!" and the four of us buried our junk food contraband under the veils in the tub. We stood in silence, waiting for the guillotine to drop as the Postulant Mistress approached.

Sister Tons-of-Fun (my nickname for the Postulant Mistress) screamed, "How are the postulants going to go to evening prayer? Your procrastination created this problem. Solve it immediately!"

One of the postulants said, "We could go to chapel without veils just this once."

"Absolutely not!"

Another postulant suggested, "We could stay in the recreation hall for night prayer."

"Absolutely not!"

Finally she and I locked eyes and horns. "We could tie our aprons on our heads," I suggested.

I hit the jackpot! Sister Tons-of-Fun looked shocked once again. The postulants proceeded to chapel with aprons masquerading as veils. The four of us stayed in the basement to wash, dry and iron the veils into the early hours of the morning.

Before leaving the basement, I called a meeting of the four of us, though the bell had already rung for profound silence. This was a very strict rule wherein every Sister had to keep silence as well as "custody of the eyes" throughout the night. This meant your vision could not extend higher than the floor. Nobody ever explained the purpose of profound silence or custody of the eyes. I presumed it had something to do with increasing privacy while preparing for bed and decreasing relationships during the night. I instructed the three postulants to keep profound silence and custody of the eyes as I conducted the meeting regarding confession of faults.

I believe an explanation of the ritual of confession of faults is in order. A postulant would kneel in front of the Postulant Mistress and reiterate all the things she did wrong during the week. It was exactly like going to a priest for confession and receiving penance, which consisted of saying a certain number of prayers. While there is a difference between a major sin and a minor fault, there was also a very important similarity: both were written in stone. No matter what I confessed in either ritual, everything was punishable by saying six Hail Marys and six Our Fathers.

I explained to the three other postulants it was imperative that each of us confess our faults with consistency rather than honesty. I told them I planned to confess that I did not schedule my time well when washing and ironing the veils. I was not going to confess to stealing the Cokes and cookies. Since we didn't eat or drink much, I figured we didn't have to confess much. That minor detail would slip into the cosmos beyond the point of retrieval. Since the episode in the basement never came up again, I assume the three postulants followed my game plan.

Of the one hundred twenty-two postulants who entered in my group, one hundred and one remained to make Reception and become novices. We were the largest group to ever receive the habit as Adrian Dominicans. As Reception Day grew closer, each postulant was given a mound of white mohair fabric that she would morph into a traditional Dominican habit. Bringing form and function to this fabric was the final hurdle in the rite of passage from postulant to novice.

Only five days remained before Reception Day and I wondered why I had yet to receive my bolt of material. One hundred postulants had received the necessary supplies and training to make their habits, and still I'd been given nothing. I went to the novice in charge of helping postulants make their habits and inquired about my situation. She knew nothing and most certainly would not inquire on my behalf.

As we began practicing for reception into the novitiate, I still had no material for my habit. With Reception Day growing closer, I began to realize the seriousness of my situation. At the end of recreation, Sister Tons-of-Fun held up the last pile of fabric and announced that, once she gave it out, everyone would have the needed supplies to make their habits. When she handed me the torch, everyone clapped. I couldn't believe it; nobody ever received applause for anything. Everyone had been given their material without fanfare. As I hugged the fabric, I knew I had made it to the next level, but I still had no idea how I was going to sew an entire habit in a single day. In that moment I sorely missed the luxury of having my mother's seamstresses at my disposal.

After night prayer, I ran to the sewing room and found the last few postulants in the final stages of habit-making. The profound silence bell rang, and I panicked, realizing I couldn't talk with the novice who was helping the postulants with their sewing.

I wrote her a note: "How do you plug in the machine?"

She wrote back, "There's no plug. Use your feet." I looked down and saw other postulants jogging in place as they sewed their habits! I panicked, thinking to myself *are you kidding me? I'm the daughter of Catherine Bisignano.* My mom loved antiques, but she never owned a sewing machine attached to an exercise bike.

I wrote another note: "Never mind. Let's just take a habit off a dead nun!"

She laughed and wrote back: "We can accomplish this. Let's get busy."

To this day, I don't know the name of that novice, but in that moment, I felt I owed her my life and whatever was left of my sanity.

We worked all night. When I did not go to the dorm, other postulants snuck out and met us in the sewing room. Each postulant helped me put together a piece of the habit. Some postulants used two machines to sew simultaneously on a single piece of fabric. I sewed simple hems that didn't show. By noon the next day, after all-night lessons in humility and gratitude, I was ready to make the transition from postulant to novice.

Thank you, Sisters.

The Novitiate

The novitiate is the second phase of the formation process. Novices spend a year in prayer and study at the motherhouse, our home facility. Being a novice is more intense than being a postulant. The novices lead the daily chanting of Matins, Lauds and Vespers in Latin with hundreds of Sisters in the motherhouse chapel. It was a big deal—similar to learning Hebrew for a Bar or Bat Mitzvah. If you couldn't lead the daily Latin chant, you did not make profession, that is, you did not take temporary vows of poverty, chastity and obedience as an Adrian Dominican.

When I became a novice, I was given the name Sister John Catherine. My youngest brother is John, my sister was Mary Kay (Catherine) and my mom was Catherine. I liked the name, and I felt it fit me well. I wore the white Dominican habit as a badge of honor. I looked like a nun, walked like a nun, and talked like a nun, so I decided finally that I must be a nun.

In monastic times, schola was a musical school attached to a monastery or church. Today, schola refers to a group of musicians specializing in liturgical music and, more specifically, Gregorian chant. Every novice at our motherhouse wanted to sing in schola. There were about twelve available spots, which gave me about a ten percent chance to gain admittance to this prestigious group. I was not going to be denied a place in schola. I handled the audition like tryouts for a basketball team—offering to play a position few people wanted. Almost everyone wanted to sing soprano, a few wanted to sing second, but nobody wanted to sing alto. An alto I would be.

I listened from the hallway for two days as novices auditioned for schola. Everyone had to sing *O Sacrum Convivium* as the Director played the piano.

The Director kept shouting, "Louder. Louder."

I quickly got the idea that quantity (volume) was more important than quality (pitch). When it was my turn I entered the room and said, "Is this where I audition for the orchestra?"

The nun looked surprised and said, "No. Were you in an orchestra?"

I quickly replied, "Yes." I had played the violin for fourteen years and was first violinist in my high school orchestra. I sensed this was my opportunity to distinguish myself and, as was my nature, I seized the moment.

"So you read music?"

"Yes."

"Do you play well?"

"Yes, but I have a hard time with fifth position (the highest and hardest fingering on the violin) and double stops (playing two strings at the same time), and I always played too loudly."

"What songs did you play?"

"Well, every Christmas we played The Hallelujah Chorus from Händel's Messiah."

"Nice."

I hadn't sung a note and I knew I was in schola. Getting into schola was the easiest game I ever played—I mean, the easiest audition I ever had. To this day, I still remember the hymn I sang:

O Sacrum Convivium was written by Saint Thomas Aquinas, a Dominican theologian in 1794. The hymn expresses the mystery and miracle of Jesus present in the Eucharist:

O sacrum convivium!	O sacred banquet!
in quo Christus sumitur:	in which Christ is received,
recolitur memoria passionis eius:	the memory of his Passion is recalled,

mens impletur gratia:	our souls are filled with grace,
et futurae gloriae nobis pignus datur.	and the pledge of future glory is given to us.
Alleluia.	Alleluia.

Our Sisters own and operate Siena Heights University (Adrian, Michigan) located on our motherhouse campus. A week after schola auditions, the director of the Siena Heights orchestra asked to see me.

"So you play the violin?" she asked.

"Yes, Sister." Now I knew I was in trouble. I usually told people I played the violin for four years—not fourteen—so when I played, they would be impressed.

She asked, "Will you play for me?"

I asked, "Will you accompany me on the piano?" She stared at me like she had every right to ask me to play but I had no right to ask her to do the same.

"Yes, Sister, I will."

I always played well with piano accompaniment because I adjusted the sharps and flats to the tones of the piano. In other words, with piano accompaniment, I could play the violin in tune.

The nun asked, "What would you like to play?"

"I see you have Brahms on your piano. How about Hungarian Dance No. 5?"

I knew the piece by heart and was confident in playing it, although I had not practiced in several months.

After nailing Brahms, the nun asked "Will you play in the orchestra?"

I replied, "May I please use my own violin?"

She said, "Where is your violin?"

I raised the violin in my hands.

I said, "This is the apprentice-made Stradivarius that I brought with me when I first entered as a postulant. My parents bought it for me when I became first violinist in the high school orchestra. It disappeared when I got here, and I have been wondering where it went."

The nun was visibly uncomfortable. I added, "I have no future as a violinist. I am glad my violin found its way to a better place and player." The tension broke.

She said, "Yes, Sister, you may use my violin—our violin—in the orchestra." I responded with the proper phraseology:

"May God reward you, Sister."

As I returned to the novitiate, I accepted this quick lesson in detachment from material things. To this day, however, I am disappointed to have lost my violin to a better place and player. I hope my—our—Stradivarius still sits on the piano of the director of the orchestra at Siena Heights University, where it belongs.

Novices were allowed to study certain subjects such as theology, philosophy, cosmology, English, history, etc. We were not allowed to study the sciences or the arts, schola and orchestra excluded. I think this restriction had more to do with the extra hours required in labs and studios than actual course content. I never sought an explanation and no clarification was ever given. I wanted to study biology, chemistry and physics. That, however, would have to wait until after First Profession.

I absolutely loved philosophy. I immersed myself in the ancient works of Aristotle and Plato. As a young novice, I imagined sitting in an Athens marketplace asking questions of Socrates, who responded with questions of his own. I later transitioned to medieval philosophers and theologians: Albert the Great, Thomas Aquinas and Augustine. After that, the modern thinkers: René Descartes, Immanuel Kant, Søren Kierkegaard, Karl Marx, Friedrich Nietzsche, Jean-Jacques Rousseau, Jean-Paul Sartre, Baruch Spinoza and Voltaire.

Today, I study Buddhism seasoned with Confucianism and Taoism. I immerse myself in the works of spiritual masters: Lao-Tzu, Buddha, Jesus, Gurdjieff, Krishnamurti and Thích Nhất Hạnh. Through these spiritual and philosophical resources I am now convinced that life is best lived through deep, consistent prayer and meditative practices.

Though I have lived a life dedicated to education, I still have dreams with regards to my own learning. I often think about the possibility of praying and studying with Pema Chödrön, the first American woman ordained a Buddhist nun in 1981. Five years later, she became head of the Gampo Abbey in Nova Scotia, Canada, the first Tibetan Buddhist monastery in North America for Western men and women. Chödrön teaches a rain retreat at Gampo Abbey every winter and spends her summers teaching on the Guide to the Bodhisattva's Way of Life in Berkeley. She spends seven months a year in solitary retreat. I participate in Pema's online courses. I would love to sit and talk with her in person.

I also yearn to pray and study with Jetsün Khandro Rinpoche, a female Tibetan Buddhist lama born in Kalimpong, India. She speaks fluent English and has taught in Europe, North America and Southeast Asia since 1987. She established and heads the Samten Tse Retreat Centre in Mussoorie, India—a place of study and prayer for Eastern nuns and Western lay practitioners living together in spiritual community. Currently, about fifty Buddhist nuns and thirty western students reside at Samten Tse. Certainly they have room for a retired Dominican nun longing for prayerful solitude. Khandro Rinpoche also founded and teaches at Lotus Garden Retreat Center in Stanley, Virginia. Sangha members, monks, nuns and noble ones from around the world travel to Lotus Garden to receive teachings from Rinpoche, to undertake personal retreats and study Tibetan Buddhism.

One of my dreams before I die is to spend time studying and praying with Pema Chödrön and Khandro Rinpoche. That would mean more to me than my four degrees ever have. The lifelong lessons of love and kindness towards myself and others, obtained through opportunities presented in everyday life, are far more precious to me than any formal higher education.

Standing for Justice

I am incredibly grateful to the ongoing leadership within the Adrian Dominican Sisters who allowed and encouraged me to develop an early, ongoing sense of social justice. One particular ritual in the novitiate had a profound influence on my values, positions and actions. The all-night-vigils in which I participated fifty years ago influence me to this day.

Whenever any of our nuns were in life-threatening situations, the novices were summoned to the motherhouse chapel for a prayer vigil. We were briefly told the circumstances that endangered our Sisters, then divided into pairs and assigned hourly time slots. We prayed continuously—all day and all night—until the crisis dissipated. The prayers of the novices encouraged our Sisters to take public stands for justice and peace, and those in danger gave the novices the opportunity to stand in solidarity with them. I especially remember two prayer vigils during my novitiate years.

The first involved several of our Sisters who were stationed at our *Colegio* (high school) in Santo Domingo in the Dominican Republic from 1940–1974. Rafael Trujillo, president of the Dominican Republic from 1930–38 and 1942–52, exercised absolute power. Even after he left office, he continued to rule through puppet presidents like his brother. Trujillo was renowned for his oppression and abuse of human rights. Preoccupied with "whitening" the Dominican population, he exploited Haitians who worked, stayed and started families in the Dominican Republic. He had twenty thousand Haitian peasants killed his first year in office. The bishops in the Dominican Republic consistently and publicly condemned Trujillo for his ongoing genocidal actions.

In May of 1961, we received word the Bishop of Santo Domingo was under arrest for treason against the government. Trujillo's army refused to raid the convent or spray the school with bullets because our Sisters hid the Bishop in the convent. For days, our nuns protected and defended Bishop Pittini Piussi of Santo Domingo against the forces of Rafael Trujillo. Trujillo was murdered by his own armed forces on May 30, 1961. The Bishop returned to his work in Santo Domingo.

The second situation occurred in March of 1965, when African-Americans decided to walk from Selma to Montgomery, Alabama in defense of their voting rights. At the time, Lowndes County, located between the two cities, was eighty-one percent African-American, but not a single one was registered to vote. Civil rights organizers had no idea that this demonstration would mark the political and emotional peak of the American Civil Rights Movement. Martin Luther King, Jr. solicited the support of civil rights activists, and our Sisters became vigorous participants. The first rally took place on Sunday, March 7, 1965. Immediately, local police with billy clubs and tear gas attacked six hundred protesters.

The following Monday, the novices began a prayer vigil in support of our Sisters who would be walking arm-in-arm with Martin Luther King, Jr. This time, the twenty-five hundred demonstrators planned to march to the Edmund Pettus Bridge, cross the bridge and hold a prayer service before returning to Selma. A court injunction prevented them from going any further. That night, three white ministers were attacked and beaten with clubs. One of them died after the Selma public hospital refused to treat his injuries.

On March 21, 1965, over eight thousand people assembled in Selma to commence the fifty mile march to Montgomery. When the highway narrowed to two lanes, the law allowed only three hundred protesters, including our Sisters, to continue on. They walked ten miles a day and camped along the road each evening. On March 24, as the three hundred protesters entered the city of Montgomery, they were again joined by thousands of supporters.

Throughout the march, a total of four thousand U.S. Army soldiers, Alabama National Guard members under Federal command, FBI agents and Federal Marshals accompanied the protesters without a single incident of harassment by the police or segregation supporters. This third peaceful march increased public support for the Civil Rights Movement. In 1965, President Lyndon Johnson presented a bill to a joint session of Congress which later became the Voting Rights Act. Looking back, I remember the vigils we held as some of my proudest moments during my time as a novice. It was empowering to know that, in prayer and spirit, we were contributing to the change our country so desperately needed.

The 1960s seemed like the perfect time to promote social change amidst profound inconsistencies. As an Adrian Dominican, I was afforded a platform from which I could embrace activism and function within the emerging sociopolitical revolution of the 1960s. At the same time, however, I was reluctant to perpetuate abusive traditions in religious life. I rebelled against blind obedience, public humiliation and the belief that brokenness was the key to holiness. I could not accept the contradiction between the way those in authority oppressed my Sisters and our mission to promote social justice, peace and understanding through our good works.

If radical changes had not occurred within the Catholic Church in the 1960s, I would not be a nun today. The Second Vatican Council, known as Vatican II, addressed relations between the Catholic Church and the modern world. It opened under Pope John XXIII in 1962 and closed under Pope Paul VI in 1965. Pope John XXIII wanted to promote better understanding of the whole of humankind as being part of God's plan for the world. When asked about the purpose of Vatican II, he replied simply, "It is time to open the windows and to let some fresh air into the Church." He went on to launch the Second Vatican Council in a remarkably warm atmosphere and impress the world with his own humanity.

Ironically, I found my niche within religious life not from the Catholic Church, but from my membership in the Adrian Dominican Congregation. They accepted my craving for prayer, community and service. They tolerated my longing for a personal identity. Today, they reluctantly support my quest to connect with Pachamama and her Earth community in the Amazon Jungle. It was providential that I sought membership into the Adrian Dominican Congregation during formative times for both of us. Because we changed together, I did not have to "drop out" of religious life as a matter of integrity.

Unfortunately, social change within religious life never occurred fast enough to satisfy my desire to enact change in my world. I wanted mutual respect for and among my Sisters. One minute, I was standing in solidarity with my Sisters as we confronted social injustices and the next minute I was quite literally eating off the floor as punishment for my headstrong nature. No abuse I encountered within my experience of religious life devalued a person more than the practice of floor dishes, which consisted of sitting on the floor to eat because you were deemed unworthy of sitting at the table with the other Sisters. I often committed the "mortal sin" of smiling at, nodding to or momentarily speaking with professed Sisters. A professed Sister was one who graduated from the novitiate and was under temporary or final vows. When I confessed having spoken with them, my sentence was, more often than not, a floor dish.

Our meals were eaten in silence as a novice read the work of a contemporary theologian over a microphone. The protocol for a floor dish consisted of putting your legs out straight, not crossed at the ankles or bent at the knees, while you held an empty plate and fork in your lap. If novices or professed Sisters thought you were entitled to eat, they placed food on your plate as they desired. You could not get up and walk around and ask your friends for food. You were required to sit stationary as the nuns seated nearby handed you food from their table.

Nuns new to the abuse of floor dishes thought it was important to have their backs supported during the meal. They situated themselves beside the pillars in the refectory (dining hall). I saw this as a strategic mistake since the pillars were not positioned near the dining tables. Once a rookie floor-disher sought the false comfort of a cement pillar, she was stuck without a nearby food source. I, on the other hand, was an expert in the art of floor dishes. It was critical that you relinquished a comfortable position for a strategic location next to tables occupied by the retired Sisters. The old nuns had the best food and the most compassion. Their bread pudding NEVER had peas in it.

I was always looking out for poor, inexperienced novices who took floor dishes next to pillars. Once, when a Sister was not getting any food, I quickly piled my plate and took it to her. The Novice Mistress motioned to speak with me.

She whispered, "Would you like to take her place?"

I jumped enthusiastically on her sarcasm. "Yes. May God reward you, Sister."

Before she could explain herself, I was kneeling by the novice telling her to take my place at the table while I took her spot on the floor. I got another floor dish for that act of dinner disobedience.

The next day, I sat on the floor directly beside the Novice Mistress. When she offered me food, I said, "No thank you, Sister." Knowing that she was hard of hearing, I continued by shouting, "MY MOTHER TOLD US NEVER TO FEED THE DOGS AT THE TABLE!" I went on a hunger strike as she choked down the rest of her meal. She never gave me another floor dish.

Every postulant and novice had a daily chore called an *obedience*. Obediences separated the sheep from the goats. If you were tall and slender and floated like an angel when you walked, you were appointed a *sacristan*, the keeper of sacred objects. We called the sacristans "dollies." They cleaned the sanctuary—the section of the chapel that contained the altar and tabernacle (enclosure for the Eucharist). Sacristans lit the candles for daily Mass as every Sister in the motherhouse gazed upon their grace and beauty. With two of the three traits, you were still a winner. You got to clean the rest of the chapel, but you were not allowed to get close to the candelabras.

Most of the time, my obedience was to clean an obscure bathroom in a remote part of campus. Once I was assigned a high profile obedience, when I was handed a toothbrush and told to clean the white marble stairs in the main lobby of the motherhouse. At the bottom of the stairs was a life size crucifix with a dead Jesus hanging from it. The top of His foot was worn and shiny because each Sister touched it as she passed. As I stared at Jesus, I wondered if my humiliation was part of the world He had hoped and preached for.

On the landing between the first and second floors of the motherhouse, there was a huge statue of an angel holding a gold chalice. I think it was Archangel Michael because he was dressed for battle while holding a sword. Once I was cleaning the statue while eating an apple. Apples were no longer considered forbidden fruit within the Garden of Eden, however novices were forbidden to eat between meals. From the landing, I spotted the Novice Mistress bow toward the crucifix and turn to ascend the marble stairs. I immediately tossed the apple into Saint Michael's chalice! I never retrieved it. If I ever return to the motherhouse, I am going to track down Michael and inspect his chalice for apple seeds.

The absolute best obedience I ever had was feeding the nuns at the infirmary. Each day at noon I took trays to nuns marooned in their rooms, as they were unable to get to the dining hall. I told each Sister she had gotten the first tray on the floor because I wanted to make sure her meal remained hot. She was not to discuss this secret with any of the other Sisters on the floor because I did not want the others to know that she was receiving special treatment. As far as I know my deception was never uncovered.

The biggest privilege I had in the novitiate was the honor of feeding Sister Marcus, who was confined to bed. She could not move a single muscle from her neck down. No one ever told me her story. Novices were not allowed to ask. With effort, Sister Marcus slowly and softly spoke with amazing joy and clarity. I felt it was far more of a privilege to feed Sister Marcus than it would be to light all the candelabras in St. Peter's Basilica in Rome.

Sister Marcus loved ice cream. We served ice cream on Sundays, but I made sure that Sister Marcus got ice cream every day. She often got brain freezes from eating too fast, and she always wanted to get rid of the ice cream carton as quickly as possible. Though she appreciated the gesture, I think she was afraid I would get in trouble for bending the rules in her favor. I stood silently in the corner of the room when Sister Marcus died, surrounded by our Sisters. While I have had the privilege of escorting many souls to a higher level of consciousness, hers was the most special passing I ever experienced.

Thank you, Sister Marcus.

Not every meal in the infirmary was as peaceful an experience as with Sister Marcus. I fed another nun confined to bed called Sister R. who, unlike Sister Marcus, was quite capable of movement. She would thrash uncontrollably, making loud guttural sounds while trying to free her arms, as she had been strapped firmly to the railing of her bed. In my opinion, if there is a hell on Earth, this nun was in it. She probably should have been in a padded cell with a trained attendant, and despite our best intentions, our infirmary and my skills, we were unable to assist her efficiently.

These were my instructions: "Feed Sister R., but never, ever remove her restraints. She is extremely violent. If she escapes, she will hurt someone." Looking into the eyes of this Sister felt to me like staring into the eyes of a hungry tiger. Lost for words, I often hummed as I fed her. One day she was making a soft noise while eating and I asked the nurse, "Is she okay?"

The nurse replied, "Yes, she's alright. She is trying to hum along with you."

I was overjoyed; it seemed to me that this was a real breakthrough. One day I asked Sister R. if she wanted me to sing to her. She responded with a soft growl that I took to be, "Yes." Every day I sang the songs I knew, which were mostly just the alto sections of schola songs. She didn't seem to mind and I certainly needed the practice.

As months passed, I learned how to converse with Sister R. in my own way. It started out as a monologue, but every time I paused, Sister R. would gurgle something. I waited for her to finish and said, "Exactly. You said…"

and I would add something to the conversation as if two people were actually conversing. We began to have amazing, detailed conversations. We discussed the works of the greatest minds in theology, cosmology and philosophy. Sometimes we just gossiped about the other nuns, especially those down the hall in the infirmary.

One of my most distinct memories of Sister R. happened on Easter Sunday. I was wearing my new habit—the one made by a gang of postulants. As I greeted Sister R., I told her it was Easter.

"Do you like my Easter outfit?"

Sister R. responded with one of her trademark gurgles.

I said, "Thank you. I made it all by myself!"

Then I made a serious mistake. I told Sister R., since it was Easter Sunday, I was going to remove her wrist restraints while she ate dinner. Things were going well. She gestured that she wanted to hold the glass of tomato juice. She took a sip, then flailed the glass at me. There we were, both covered in tomato juice! My collar was saturated. The collar on the habit flares from the neck, wraps around the back, arms and chest, and stops at the elbows and waist.

I immediately restrained Sister R., took off my collar and soaked it in her sink. I tried to feed Sister R., but her demeanor changed and she wouldn't eat. She screamed and flailed around, trying to free herself. As I was changing her top sheet, a nurse came in to see what the commotion was about. I said, "There has been a little accident." The nurse hit Sister R. in the face. I quickly grabbed the nurse's arm and yelled, "Stop. If you ever hit her or any other nun, I'll report you to those in authority. This is not Sister R.'s fault. It is my fault. I took off her restraints and handed her a glass of tomato juice. She did not have the coordination to hold the glass. It slipped." Sister R. immediately settled down. I said, "See? Sister R. knows this is exactly what happened." The nurse stomped out of the room.

I continued my duties at the infirmary without wearing my collar. All I had was the scapular that hung from my shoulders over my tunic. It was obvious I was out of uniform. The Superior of the infirmary asked to see me. I told the Superior the same story. I didn't tell her about the nurse who hit Sister

R., though I probably I should have. I got on my knees and pleaded, "I know you are not my Superior. I know I should report this incident to the Novice Mistress. If I do, I will be reassigned to clean the bathrooms in De Profundus Hall. Please give me a penance so we can call all this even." The Superior told me to stand up and bring her my collar. When I returned, she handed me one of her own collars. We were about the same size. The material and shade of white matched my scapular and tunic perfectly. She told me my collar would be hanging in her office the next day.

As I was leaving her office, the Superior said, "Sister John Catherine, thank you for treating the nuns in the infirmary with respect. Thank you for the conversations you offer them."

I responded, "May God reward you, Sister, but that's the easy part of my job."

Before returning to the novitiate, I swiped a handful of homemade cookies and a glass of cold milk from the infirmary kitchen. As Sister R. ate the snack, I told her how amazing her Superior had been to me. I moved close to her and whispered, "I am sorry I ruined your Easter dinner. Thank you for treating me with respect. Thank you for the conversations you offer me." As I gazed into her eyes, they slowly filled with tears.

Thank you, Sister R.

Mercywood Sanitarium

Before long, the darker side of religious life began to take its toll on me. I remained caught under the suffocating weight of my new life, and I watched as new rituals unfurled before me…asking permission to take a bath and wash my clothes, saying endless rosaries while kneeling with my arms outstretched. I just didn't get it. I was convinced the treatment I received was temporary, and would end with my gaining the respect of my Sisters. Besides, no "superior" could scream louder than my mother. It was a softer, gentler time than my childhood, so I watched and waited, telling myself it would soon get better.

I remember thinking: *This can't be real. It must be a test—and I'll be damned if I am going to fail it! Maybe it's even a joke. Why must people be broken before declaring them whole? Where is the holiness in humiliation? When did humiliation replace humility? I know the women I admired at St. Augustine's in Des Moines were genuine. I will persevere until I am one of them.*

If I made it through the novitiate year, I would be sent "on mission" where I knew the nuns were real and life was normal. I had witnessed their caring community with my own eyes for fourteen years. It was the only thing I could trust. I grew more and more disillusioned with the abuses inflicted on myself and my peers. I regretted not complaining to those in authority, knowing that would have been the just and honorable thing to do. Instead, I reached out to the novices who were consistently abused. I broke silence—even the "profound silence" of the night—to whisper to them that they were marvelous. They deserved better. They *were* better. We laughed at the absurdity of authority gone wild.

Little did I know I was about to be confronted with one of the most horrendous experiences of my life. One day, I woke up with double vision. The Novice Mistress said I would be taken to Toledo to see an eye doctor. When I got to Toledo, the nun who was driving told me to wait in the car. She told me she had to see a nun who was sick in the hospital before she took me to my appointment. Everything sounded normal to me, and I waited patiently in the car. Several minutes later, I was pulled from the car, forced up the stairs of Mercywood Sanitarium, and admitted as a mental patient in an insane asylum! No intake conversation, no paperwork, no signature, no diagnosis, and no explanation. I had no idea what was happening. I was paralyzed with fear and instinctively knew that I was in for the fight of my life, while completely on my own.

The next day, Dr. Berrah came to my room and asked if I knew why I was there.

I said, "I think it might be because I have double vision."

He said, "Your Novice Mistress thinks you have double vision because you are having a vicarious experience relative to your sister dying with Hodgkin's disease." He asked, "What do you think?"

I responded, "I am not living my sister's illness! I think my Novice Mistress is the crazy one and should be here rather than me."

Dr. Berrah threw his head back and laughed. I thought I had just made a friend, but I didn't trust him and explained that I had to return to the novitiate immediately. If ten days elapsed away from the motherhouse, I would have to repeat my novitiate year. Dr. Berrah explained that he was instructed to keep me for six weeks while he observed my reaction to "breaking my canonical year."

He then asked me, "How does this make you feel?"

I said, "I feel very angry. Who is in charge here, you or my Novice Mistress?"

He said, "Your Novice Mistress."

I knew I was in trouble. I resolved to return to that mental survival mode I had known and practiced so much, and began concentrating on everyone and everything but me.

Recently I Googled Mercywood Sanitarium. I found that it opened in 1924 and closed in 1986. It was demolished for some reason I could not discover. I thought I had been taken to Toledo, Ohio, yet was actually in Ann Arbor, Michigan.

I suspect that, because I was wearing the Dominican habit, the patients in Mercywood Sanitarium thought I was a staff member at the hospital. They kept coming to me for assistance and I obliged every way I could. I fed them, bathed them, walked them, entertained them, and cleaned and repaired their rooms. I remember one woman in particular who was disturbed beyond the point of communication or interaction. I kept my eye on her, as I wanted to make sure she would not harm herself or any of the other patients. I checked on her one day and found that she had swallowed her fist. She died in my arms. That day I signed out for chapel, but took a detour to the gym. I played basketball for hours.

I had two personal goals while at Mercywood: to avoid medication and electroshock therapy. I watched as patients received electroshock therapy. It is a horrible, inhumane protocol, and was administered even more liberally back then than it is today. As for the pills, I hid them under my tongue while I swallowed the water. After collecting several hundred pills I returned them to Dr. Berrah, who immediately discontinued all further medication. I asked Dr. Berrah if I was scheduled for electroshock therapy. He said, "Absolutely not." I must have looked terrified at worst and skeptical at best because he added, "People who do not need medication do not need electroshock therapy."

One day I received a phone call from Mom and Dad, who were both crying. My first thought was that Mary Kay had died, and my heart sank. However, I was surprised to discover they were crying for me. I had never experienced their concern on such a deep level. Dad said he would be there the next day to demolish the hospital brick by brick until he found me. I begged him not to interfere. I told him that if he did something "crazy" I would not be allowed to make profession as an Adrian Dominican.

Mom said to me, "I'm sorry, Judy."

I said, "For what?"

She said, "For a lot of things."

Finally, my six-week sentence was up. I felt like a death row inmate who had been given an eleventh hour reprieve. Before Dr. Berrah said goodbye he asked if I would listen to the letter he wrote to the Mother General of the Congregation, as well as my Novice Mistress. He wrote that a horrible mistake had been made—perhaps on a criminal level. Except for the resilience of Sister John Catherine, great harm and irreparable damage could have been inflicted on this eighteen-year-old. He said he would never again take an Adrian Dominican into Mercywood Sanitarium without first examining the Sister. He questioned the skills and motives of the people who decided I needed psychiatric care. He even suggested they might be delusional and in need of care themselves and mentioned that those who sent me come and see him.

I told Dr. Berrah I was very angry and returning to the motherhouse with his letter was a bittersweet victory.

He said, "What should I have done?"

"You should have stopped the abuse and, as every day elapsed, you chose not to do so. You are more a victim within your system than I will ever be in mine."

I never saw or heard from Dr. Berrah again.

When I returned to the motherhouse, the Novice Mistress said, "Sister John Catherine, you seem to have forgotten that when you return from seeing the doctor, you kneel and thank me for having sent you."

I knelt and said, "May God reward you, Sister, for sending me to the doctor."

I stood up, walked away and irately began my second novitiate.

As I began my second year, I was determined to prove I could finish the monumental undertaking of becoming an Adrian Dominican. It was two days before Profession, the day the novices take temporary vows. I would have both feet in the door during this five-year probationary period. In two days,

I would either stay at the motherhouse to continue my college studies or go "on mission." I prayed I would be sent on mission. I thought to myself, *I'll go anywhere, please God, don't keep me here.*

The Novice Mistress called me into her office and said, "I think you should see a doctor. If you get a clean bill of health, you can make Profession." I wasn't worried. I knew I wasn't sick.

That afternoon, the doctor I saw told me, "You have a node on your thyroid. Come and see me after Profession and we will dissolve it. Thyroid tumors are rarely cancerous." He then called my Novice Mistress and told her I would be a medical risk if I was allowed to make Profession.

My brother Jim, who was living in Detroit, was summoned to the motherhouse in Adrian. We arrived at the same time, and I was transferred from the motherhouse car into Jim's car. I was gone in seconds. The Novice Mistress said something to Jim but I did not catch the comment. Jim shouted, "Go to hell!" That was the only time I'd ever heard my brother curse.

Forced Exit from the Convent

My parents met me at Mayo Clinic in Rochester, Minnesota. It was confirmed I had a lump on my thyroid. They operated. It was cancer. They removed my thyroid, parathyroid and thymus glands. Ironically, the doctor commented, "I'm surprised you didn't have double vision. It is often seen in cases like yours."

My mom came into the room, crying. Again, I assumed my sister had died.

I asked, "Why are you crying?"

She said, "Mary Kay has cancer. You have cancer. I have cancer. What are we going to do?" At that moment I witnessed, for the first time, the suffering of my mom on a very deep level. She was in excruciating emotional pain. Being my naive and verbal self, I thought she actually wanted an answer to her question.

"Mary Kay is going to die and you and I are going to get through this together." At that moment, at the age of twenty, my relationship with my mom took on new power. Nothing was ever worth fighting about again.

For the next two years, I had two goals, to act as if I was healthy and to get back into the convent. I joined the Papal Volunteers—the Peace Corp for Catholic kids. I was assigned to the village of Jesús del Monte in the mountains above Morelia in Michoacán, Mexico. I ate raw bananas for six weeks—

until my skin turned approximately the same shade of green. An elder in this remote highland village extracted my appendix with a kitchen knife while his wife, holding a hen under her arm, observed the procedure. They fed my appendix to the chicken! My parents and youngest brother, John, rescued me from a hospital-of-sorts in the town of Morelia at the bottom of the mountain.

I was surprised to hear my parents were on their way to Mexico. My dad couldn't stand the effects of extreme poverty on humanity. He informed me that Mom, John and he had taken a 250 mile taxi ride from Mexico City to Morelia! The driver was waiting outside with the motor running to take Dad back to Mexico City, where he then flew to Des Moines. Before leaving Morelia, Dad asked the taxi driver to take him to the open market. Dad bought all the fresh fruit and vegetables in the entire market, and paid two men to truck the food up the mountain to the "American kids" camping inside the church yard in Jesuś del Monte. He told them to take food for their own families as well. The "American kids" were grateful beyond words. No more turning green on bananas.

My dad's comment was priceless: "The next time you want to do good in this world, just stay home and I'll send money!"

Thanks, Dad.

I returned to Des Moines and enrolled at Clark College in Dubuque, Iowa. The college is owned and operated by the Sisters of Charity of the Blessed Virgin Mary (BVM) and is located a short ride from the BVM motherhouse. Sister Thomasette, Mary Kay's superior and our former high school teacher, told me to sneak up the back steps of the motherhouse and visit Mary Kay in her bedroom every day. This was a privilege afforded to no one. At this point, Mary Kay was bedridden. Maybe, just maybe, she was treated with kindness and respect. I never asked and she never said. She suffered terribly. I considered our time together to be a priceless opportunity to connect on a deep, personal level.

I was grateful for my newfound freedom as a college student during the turbulent decade of the 1960s. Support for the Civil Rights Movement and opposition to the war in Vietnam increased, and I joined the ranks of the defiant, raucous Baby Boomers on campus. As our parents huddled in fear over the inevitability of a Communist invasion through Cuba, we pooled our naïveté and nonconformist thinking in protesting the war and campaigning for human rights. We talked about changing the direction of society under leadership of our new president, John F. Kennedy, yet none of us could predict what the 1960s would bring for the country and the Catholic Church. While my friends got high on marijuana, I got high on civil disobedience. It was the perfect release for my anger and discontentment regarding family and religious life.

Before leaving school for Christmas break in Des Moines, I received a letter from the Mother General of the Adrian Dominicans, *"If you want to return to the novitiate, you may do so in August."* I wondered, *Where did this come from? How did this possibly happen?* I later found out my dad had asked Bishop Edward Daly, a Dominican priest and Bishop of Des Moines, to intercede on my behalf. Nothing like a famous Dominican bishop supporting an infamous Dominican novice.

I wanted very badly to be a nun, but after my initial time with the Adrian Dominicans I thought maybe instead I wanted to be a BVM. Mary Kay had a special dispensation from Pope John XXIII to join the BVMs with cancer. I was thrown out of the Adrian Dominicans with the prospect of cancer. I realized if I joined the BVMs, I would always be Mary Kay's "flawed little sister." I decided I would rather keep my reputation as a damaged Adrian Dominican. I had already made it through two novitiates, so I convinced myself I could do it a third time. After that, I would be "on mission," where I truly believed life was normal and nuns were happy.

Thanks again, Dad, and thank you, Bishop Daly.

Reentering the Novitiate

I began my third novitiate with the same Novice Mistress who sent me to the insane asylum. She didn't miss a beat. I had worn the Dominican habit, my badge of honor, less than an hour when she said, "Sister John Catherine, you seem to have forgotten that when you return from seeing the doctor, you kneel and thank me for having sent you."

Could this really be happening? It seemed insidious that she insisted upon me thanking her for sending me to the doctor. I had already thanked her for abducting and sending me to the insane asylum. Now I had to thank her for sending me home for two years? I wanted to scream, but instead, I knelt and said, "May God reward you, Sister, for sending me to the doctor."

As I stood and walked away, I again experienced profound rage. Later in life, when I sought to forgive myself and those around me for past injuries, forgiving that Novice Mistress was one of my greatest challenges.

My strategy for success for my third novitiate was simple: no asking questions, no offering comments, no staging protests, no defending or supporting others. I would keep absolute silence and total custody of the eyes for twenty-four hours a day for one year. I would do nothing that might attract notice.

Six weeks later my Novice Mistress received a call. Mary Kay was in the hospital, where she made Final Profession (took vows until death) and received the Sacrament of the Sick, at that time administered only to the dying. She had asked for me. The BVMs made a very unusual request. Even though I was a novice, they asked that I be allowed to go to Dubuque immediately. My Novice Mistress and I left for the Detroit airport within thirty minutes of the call. So much for keeping a low profile.

Although Mary Kay was barely conscious, she had worked out a scheme with my parents whereby she and I could be alone for a couple of minutes. As my Superior and I entered the room, my parents asked everyone to leave with them. My dad went to a pay phone, called the nurse's desk and said a call had come from the Adrian Dominican motherhouse for my Novice Mistress. As she left the room, Dad hung up the phone. Mary Kay and I had seconds of privacy.

She asked, "Do you want to make Profession as an Adrian Dominican?"

"Yes."

"Are you sure?"

"Yes, yes, of course."

"Then just play along with me."

She shut her eyes and rested. My Superior reentered the room and asked if we had visited. I whispered, "I think she's asleep."

Mary Kay opened her eyes and said, "I just had the most amazing vision."

My Superior took the bait.

"What was it?"

"I was at Judy's Profession. She was making her vows to Mother G. (she used the name of our major superior). You and I were standing together. Everything was white." Mary Kay looked my Novice Mistress in the eyes and whispered, "I will be coming to Judy's Profession and I will be bringing all the angels and saints from Heaven."

Personally, I thought she was laying it on a little thick, but my Novice Mistress said to Mary Kay, "I will see you at your sister's Profession." Mary Kay smiled. As my Superior turned away, Mary Kay opened her eyes and winked at me. As family and visitors poured into the room, I mused at how my sister navigated through this world during the last few days of her life. She clearly knew what she was doing in the midst of dying.

A couple of days passed and Mary Kay told me I needed to return to the motherhouse in Adrian, Michigan. She knew that if I were gone for more than ten days, I would have to make a fourth novitiate. I would return to Dubuque for her funeral. I too had calculated the days. I told Mary Kay I had two days before I had to leave.

She became very agitated and said, "No. You need those two days. You must leave now."

I could see my stubbornness upset her, so I agreed to return to the motherhouse. As I said goodbye, I knew in my heart I would never see my sister alive again.

Goodbye, Mary Kay

A week later, Mary Kay died. I was jolted from sleep and sat up in bed at 4 a.m. I knew the exact second her soul shifted because it moved over mine in passage. Mary Kay died on November 9, 1964 at the age of twenty-three, after battling Hodgkin's disease for five and one-half years. She was terminally ill for one quarter of her life.

Before leaving for Dubuque my Novice Mistress said, "Sister John Catherine, I am putting you under pain of mortal sin not to cry at your sister's funeral." This outrageous act on the part of my Novice Mistress requires an explanation.

In the past, a Superior could put an "inferior" under *pain of mortal sin* to do something or refrain from doing something. I knew the ritual existed, but I never knew it to be practiced. Supposedly, if I cried at Mary Kay's funeral, I would be committing a mortal sin, punishable by hellfire. She must have noticed the glazed look I had when she told me, so she added, "If you cry at your sister's funeral, you will not make First Profession!" Then I broke my own rule and asked a question.

"Is there something wrong with crying at a funeral?"

She said, "You are a religious woman. You must be an edification to your family and the BVMs. If you cry, it will show you have no faith." I thought to myself, *What world are you living in? How did you acquire such warped reality and theology?*

Upon arriving at the BVM motherhouse, I was met by my family, along with hundreds of nuns. My older brothers, Joe and Jim, had their wives and small children with them. Most of my nieces and nephews were too small to comprehend the finality of death. My younger brother, John, was just a kid himself. Before me stood my parents, exhausted and devastated by grief. It is an overwhelming reality when children precede their parents in death. I could see part of them had also crossed with Mary Kay. While the family seemed both distraught and relieved that her excruciating pain had ended, many of the BVMs appeared to be in disbelief, as if they had been unaware of the seriousness of her illness. They were shocked that this young nun was gone before her religious life ever began. While the older nuns seemed at peace with her passage, the younger nuns appeared to be unaware that Mary Kay had had a terminal illness.

Mary Kay's funeral was the first Mass at the BVM motherhouse to be celebrated in English rather than Latin. It was an historic event: the death of Latin and the birth of English vernacular. We replaced the exquisite music of the great sixteenth century masters with an inexperienced yet enthusiastic laity, eager to increase their leadership and participation within community.

All BVMs are buried in the cemetery on the grounds of the motherhouse. Each Sister is buried in succession according to her date of death. Mary Kay loved to meander through the cemetery and tell me the personal stories of various Sisters. Once she walked a considerable distance beyond the freshest grave. She stopped and said, "I'll be easy to find. I'll be right here, close to this old oak tree." She pointed to the tree just above her head.

At the conclusion of the funeral Mass, my dad and brothers transported the coffin from the motherhouse chapel to its final resting place in the nearby cemetery. Hundreds of Sisters, family and friends followed in procession. Sure enough, Mary Kay's journey ended under that old oak tree. I wondered how she could have known, though there was something profoundly pro-phetic about my sister. She knew and understood her destiny. Perhaps her passage through this world was brief because she fundamentally understood life; she simply *got it*. She knew who she was and leaned into her journey with acceptance and love.

I still remember my feelings as Mary Kay was lowered into the ground. While she had two parents, three brothers and hundreds of Sisters-of-sorts, I held the special place of being her only biological sister.

Thank you and goodbye, Mary Kay. I will see you soon.

Upon Mary Kay's death, all who knew her had to unlearn her expected presence in their lives. I would never again be able to sit in her bedroom at the BVM motherhouse and watch her paint. I would never again see her smile, hear her voice, smell her hair or touch her body. She would never again enter a room and fill it—and me—with warmth, tenderness and quiet concern.

I returned to the Adrian Dominican motherhouse without the skills or support to process my grief. As always, I abandoned the pain in my heart and retreated to the cluttered thoughts in my head. It may have been easier for me to relinquish Mary Kay's expected presence than anyone else because I had no experience—no anticipation—of her in my new life as an Adrian Dominican. I thought of her often, yet saw no one, went nowhere and did nothing that reminded me of her. Life was surreal. I was glad I wasn't a BVM. I didn't have to walk their halls, pass her bedroom, take their classes, eat their food, say their prayers, sing their songs and commit to furthering their goals and mission without her.

While isolation within my new environment somewhat dulled my pain, it also limited my availability and capability to assist my parents and brothers with their grief. Much of my heartache related to not being home with them and for them. Temporarily, during my third novitiate, it felt like I had lost them all. I missed each of them as much as my sister.

It was ten years before I cried; before I gave myself permission to grieve the death of my sister. Instead, I continued to guard myself with layer upon layer of anger and resentment. I refused to give myself permission to be human. I made a vow, that for as long as I lived, nothing and no one would ever touch my heart. Throughout the remainder of my novitiate, I studied hard, worked hard, prayed hard and counted the days to my Profession, where

I would publicly declare to live a vowed life as an Adrian Dominican Sister for one year.

One week prior to the Profession ceremony, I was working in the motherhouse kitchen. Sister Patrick asked me to go to the cellar and retrieve some potatoes. In all my novitiates, I did not realize the kitchen had a cellar. You practically needed a map to get there. As I descended into the musty catacomb, the mildew and stale air grabbed me by the throat, and I collapsed with an asthmatic attack, something I had not had since my childhood. It was some time before I was found, and I regained consciousness under an oxygen tent in the local hospital.

I jumped out of bed and demanded to go to the motherhouse immediately. I was told to wait for my Novice Mistress, who would be coming shortly. How long had I been in the hospital? "Several hours," I was told.

"Days or hours?"

"Hours…but you can expect to stay here for a couple of days."

Because of my trip to Dubuque it would put me at ten days away from the motherhouse. I thought of my sister, and her insistence that I leave her side so that I might have those two extra days. In that moment, I understood just how badly I would need them. How did she know?

When my Novice Mistress entered the room, I must have looked as weak as I felt. I asked her, "Did you call Jim?" She had no idea what I was talking about. I was relieved my brother Jim was not coming from Detroit to take me home again.

She said, "In a couple of days, the BVMs will be here for your Profession. I promised your sister. You need to stay here for a couple of days and get stronger."

Thanks again, Mary Kay. How did you know?

Profession Day

The BVMs came, and finally I made Profession, taking vows of poverty, chastity and obedience for one year. I was a bonafide Adrian Dominican for the next twelve months.

When the ceremony ended, the Novice Mistress told me, "Go pack. You are going on mission in two hours." Nobody ever went on mission the very day of Profession. She said, "We are sending you to Des Moines to see your parents. You will get word where to go from there."

I couldn't believe it. I was going home, not as a wash out, wipe out, loser, but as an Adrian Dominican! I was going to see my family, wearing the black veil reserved for professed nuns and novices when they went to seek medical treatment. I would be staying with the nuns at St. Augustine's, in the white mansion at the top of the hill in front of Greenwood Park lagoon. I allowed myself to entertain the idea that there might be a God afterall. My suspicions about reaching the other side of my novitiate experience seemed to be playing out. Once I made it through the novitiate, I would be able to slow down, put my feet up, and enjoy life like a normal person.

While in Des Moines, I received a postcard from the motherhouse that read: "Get on the next train and go to Albuquerque. Someone will be waiting for you." *How wonderful*, I thought to myself. I didn't have a clue where Albuquerque was located, but I knew it was far from Des Moines, Iowa and

Adrian, Michigan. The nuns at St. Augustine's said we had two schools in Albuquerque, one in the rich foothills of the Sandia Mountains and one in the barrio.

After several days on the train, I arrived in Albuquerque. Two nuns were waiting for me just like the postcard said. As we left the train station, we turned away from the mountains and headed to the barrio. Finally, I could be a voice for the poor as an Adrian Dominican Sister. This life of mine could not be better!

First Mission

I rang the bell, the door opened, and there stood the nun who had abducted and forced me into Mercywood Sanitarium! In my head I screamed, *Are you kidding me? What are the odds?*

She said, "Don't expect to be friends. You're the reason they sent me to this hellhole! I have only one thing to say to you. Don't ever be alone with the pastor. He had an affair with the last Superior. Stay away from him."

The new Superior walked in and said, "Welcome, Sister John Catherine, the pastor wants to see you!"

I went to the rectory to meet the pastor. He was drunk. I knew drunk. My dad had taught me all about it. He asked, "Have you heard anything about me?"

I said, "No, Father. Have you heard anything about me?" We laughed.

Then and there I established strong boundaries. "I'm here to teach. I'm under temporary vows. I don't want any attention or trouble." He asked if I would coach all the teams and direct the children's choir. I was an athlete. I could read music. I was qualified enough, so I said, "Sure, as long as the girls can play on the boys' teams." There were no teams for girls at that time.

He agreed and added, "We will have to work together closely with the choir."

I said, "I work alone. Either you run the choir or I run the choir." From day one, I made sure he kept a respectful distance from me, but I never respected him.

I was a decent teacher in spite of the fact that I had not yet graduated from college and knew absolutely nothing about teaching. Luckily, I had the best on-the-job training possible. I lived and worked side-by-side with some of the finest educators available. I used textbooks only as references. The kids, all Mexican-American and Native American, were the poorest in the city. They were never at their desks. We were always outside, doing science, making art, having fun, enjoying life. We took the public bus all over town in search of new discoveries. The city was our classroom. I didn't realize it at the time, but this first foray into experiential teaching set the foundation for my life's work of developing radical, alternative models of education.

In those days, young nuns were desperately needed "on mission." We finished our college degrees by taking summer school classes. It took forever to complete the coursework and lab hours for my three majors: biology, chemistry and physics.

We had the only co-ed athletic teams in the state of New Mexico. We couldn't afford jerseys, but as a symbol of pride and unity, the kids wore homemade beaded headbands that trailed down their black braids. Meanwhile, the choir grew larger than the Congregation. We made drums and percussion instruments by putting pebbles in tin cans. The choir became famous throughout New Mexico, and parishes would pay to have us sing at their Masses. When we sang wearing beaded headbands, rather than choir robes, the parishioners would say, "Hey, aren't these the kids who killed us on the basketball court last week?"

I loved the kids and I suspect they at least appreciated me for recognizing their magnificence. It was a wild, energetic, creative time. I knew I was beginning to stick out—not a good thing for a young nun with temporary vows.

Every Sunday, the nuns took turns making dinner for the group. Sunday dinner was a big deal in the convent—similar to Thanksgiving, Christmas and Easter feasts. Several weeks passed before it was my turn to cook for the nuns. Not a problem, I had this one nailed and I knew it! I used the phone (without permission), called my mom and asked her to fly Sunday dinner in for the nuns. I never even gave this a second thought. It seemed like the most normal thing to do. In looking back, I don't know why my mother ever consented to the request. I guess it actually seemed normal to her, too.

Sunday came, and I asked a nun-friend to come with me to pick up the meal. We took the car (without permission) and went to the airport baggage claim. We found it there: box after box of the most amazing Italian dinner imaginable: ravioli, spaghetti (with instruction on how to boil it), pasta fagioli (pasta-bean soup), braciole (steak rolls), homemade Italian bread, pizzelles (waffle-cookies), and bottles of red and white wine. Seemed normal to me. On the way home, I broke into the bread; my buddy broke into the wine. We were met at the door by the Superior. She was furious. All the other nuns were delighted. They couldn't wait for the next time it would be my turn to cook.

When my mom and dad came to Albuquerque to visit, my mom demonstrated great decorum. She kept protocol and stayed in the parlor. My dad burst into the living room, marched to the kitchen and began opening the refrigerator, cupboards and drawers. The Superior shouted at my dad and told him to return to the parlor. Nobody shouted at my dad; if anyone was going to be shouting, it was him. Of course, he took his sweet time making his way back to the parlor. He turned to my Superior and said, "You could learn a thing or two about hospitality from the BVMs."

Dad then reported to my mom and me, "There is no food in the refrigerator, no food in the cupboards, and no silverware in the drawer."

I said, "Dad, this is a very poor parish. There is often not enough food. That's just how it is."

He responded, "Well that's not the way it's going to be." He got up and walked out. I did not see him until late the next day, after the truck he sent arrived from the local wholesale restaurant supplier.

The driver asked me, "Where do we put the freezer?"

I said, "What freezer?"

He said, "The freezer with the cow in it!"

They delivered crate after crate of fresh fruits and vegetables; box after box of canned food. They unloaded twelve place settings with silverware, table cloths, napkins, pots and pans and every imaginable container to serve and store food. There were carving knives, coffee pots, meat cutters and machines I did not recognize. When the kitchen was packed, we filled the basement. When the basement could hold no more, we stored equipment and food in our bedrooms. I told my buddy I was going to go hide in school. I wanted to avoid the wrath of the Superior.

I heard people running down the hall to my classroom. The Superior arrived at the door and screamed, "You put them up to this!"

I responded, "What's going on?"

My buddy yelled, "Leave her alone! She didn't put anyone up to anything. We are going to keep the food. We need the food. The nuns are hungry." The Superior stormed out and returned to the convent.

I turned to my friend and said, "Don't protect me. I don't want you to get hurt."

She said, "I'm leaving this weekend."

I sensed the permanence of her statement and asked, "Leaving where? Why? When will you be back?"

She looked at me and said in a hushed voice, "I'm leaving the convent. I'm gay!"

I slumped to the ground and started to sob. I was lost in a myriad of new emotions I did not understand or anticipate. I was ill-prepared to accept the loss of this Sister—my sister. Furthermore, I was unaware of the encroaching social change that would devour me and the institution of religious life. Our "simpler yet happier way of living" was shifting to a new paradigm. I had just taken vows to live a life that was about to reinvent itself.

My father's escapade put me on probation for the rest of the year. That Superior tried to keep me from renewing my vows, which, if she succeeded, meant that I would be expelled from the Congregation. She failed! While I don't know for sure, I think the local nuns vouched for me at the motherhouse. From then on, that Superior showed obvious disdain when I was present. For some reason, I managed not to take it personally. The other nuns were delighted that this renegade Italian nun and her parents stormed the convent in Albuquerque's barrio.

The Profound Silence of Celibacy in the 1960s

I was a virgin who had taken a vow of chastity to refrain from sex with others as well as self. I assumed the same of everyone else. I was mistaken. I knew nothing about my own sexuality, let alone homosexuality or bisexuality. I was uninformed and ill-prepared to deal with the sudden disappearance of my friend, and all those who quickly followed her. One by one, two by two, my friends jumped ship. The exodus was profound and disillusioning. I would think to myself *where was this in the conversation during my three novitiates? I must have missed the meeting! Surely we had meetings about this. We had meetings about everything. But we can start the conversation now. After all, it's the late 1960s. We are all adults. We can handle this.*

Never once did I hear the words *sexuality, homosexuality* or *bisexuality* uttered in a therapeutic way within the convent. We kept profound silence. There was no forum through which to process our pain. We paid ourselves a terrible disservice, even to this day.

From my experience, homosexuality among nuns was not prevalent. It seems that some Sisters experimented for short periods of time, then recommitted to their vows. On two occasions I had Sisters waiting for me in my bed, and in both instances I chose to sleep on the living room couch. I would have made the same choice if the person had been a male. For me, it was about celibacy, not sexuality: hetero, homo or bi. I believe any woman, gay or straight, could be a nun as long as she chooses to be celibate. My friend left without ever explaining her long-term intentions.

My worst experience in the convent was listening to nuns I loved and respected come and go throughout the night. Many Sisters explored their sexuality through affairs with priests and men with whom they worked. Was anyone doing anything about this? Who was helping them with their inner conflict and confusion? Who was helping those of us who were not participating; those buried in the silence of our celibacy? The sounds of footsteps and doors interrupted the silence of the night for at least two decades. Slowly, one by one, hundreds of our Sisters left the Order. During the 1960s and 1970s, we went from twenty-four hundred members to about one thousand. They disappeared without ever saying good-bye. I grieved the loss of every one of them. Each one was my sister—a Mary Kay of sorts. Every time a nun left, I felt a portion of my soul go with her. I lost energy. I lost hope. I was scared, and deeply saddened. My childhood asthma returned, but I kept the signs of stress and depression buried deep within.

My Papal Protest

Vow of poverty notwithstanding, I was fortunate to participate in some amazing family field trips. In 1969 my parents and I went to Italy for an audience with Pope Paul VI at Castel Gandolfo, his summer villa located about fifteen miles southeast of Rome in Lazio, Italy. Castel Gandolfo is a small town of about nine thousand people occupying the Alban Hills overlooking Lake Albano. It is considered one of the most beautiful towns in Italy.

Before we left on the trip I told my mom and dad I wanted to visit Italy but had no desire to have an audience with the Pope. I asked them not to expect this of me and not to be disappointed when I refused to participate. My mom knew of my disdain for authority figures and stayed out of the argument. Dad, however, was determined to get his way. My dad was a personal friend of Mario Stopa, head of the Papal Gentlemen, laymen who assist the Pope with public affairs. Mario was in charge of protocol related to papal visits at the Vatican and Castel Gandolfo. Simply put, he determined who was granted an audience with the Pope and how close they would get to him. For some reason, Mario always carried and placed a white pillow under the Pope's feet when he sat to address visitors. I am not an authority on Vatican protocol, but I guess it's an honor to carry the papal pillow.

On previous occasions, my dad flew Mario Stopa to the United States, where he stayed at our home in Des Moines, Iowa. Needless to say, the Biz

Kids considered Mario a friend of the family rather than a friend of Pope Paul VI.

The town of Castel Gandolfo was in frenzy the morning of the audience with Pope Paul. Tickets in hand, our chauffeur, Pietro, drove us to the Pope's villa. Pietro was also a friend of the family. He drove my parents and family around whenever we were in Rome. He was as excited as everyone else.

I asked Pietro, "How many times have you had a private audience with the Pope?"

He responded humbly, "Never. Simple Italians do not get personal audiences with the Pope."

I handed Pietro my ticket and exclaimed, "They do now!"

My dad looked exasperated. He was not going to be outwitted by his devious daughter.

When we got to the villa, my dad and Mario conducted a conclave. Mario approached me and said, "You may enter the chamber without a ticket."

Pietro was standing next to my dad. While I wasn't all that impressed with the Pope, it was an absolute delight to see the joy on Pietro's face as he smiled at Pope Paul and kissed his ring. It was truly a magical moment.

After the ceremony, Mario joined us in the limousine as we headed for his favorite restaurant in Rome. When my dad invited Pietro to join us for dinner, Mario explained in Italian that it was not proper for a chauffeur to dine with a Papal Gentleman.

My dad responded, "Tonight we are all *simple Italians*."

That night I thanked my dad and told him how proud I was of him. He said the same about me. I was shocked.

I said, "Aren't you mad I gave my ticket to Pietro?"

He said, "No. Your mother warned me that you would do that. I was happy you saw the Pope without a ticket and without offending Mario."

The next day, on the way to the airport, Pietro asked if he could take us by his home to meet his very pregnant wife. They made a request of my parents. "Next week we will be having our first child. We ask your permission to name our daughter Maria Catharina after your daughter, Mary Kay." My parents were overwhelmed.

Arizona: My Answer to Everything!

My provincial, Sister John Joseph, was an amazing woman. She acted from a position of compassion and empathy. For some reason she spontaneously decided to transfer me out of the hellhole convent in Albuquerque, New Mexico to Tucson, Arizona. There I would find two nuns—one named Jean and one named Jeanne—who would be good to and for me. Sister John Joseph was right.

Sister Jean Therese Audretsch and Sister Jeanne O'Laughlin were amazing women. We laughed together, prayed together and worked ourselves to death. They loved my parents and my folks loved them. Sister Jean Therese was appointed the Superior of the house. Her philosophy was: "You have permission to do anything that allows you to grow as a person and Dominican. You decide."

Sister Jean Therese and others appointed in the mid-1970s represented the last of the old time Superiors, but I don't think so. To me they represented a new kind of Superior who had self-respect that translated into respect for others. They treated us like the adults we were—women with each other; women in service to others. They allowed us to develop our individuality, yet brought us together in solidarity to embrace new definitions of community life and ministry.

❦

I taught junior high math and science. My teaching style had become unconventional to say the least: no desks, texts, homework, tests, or grades. I sculpted my classroom after British primary schools. I traveled to England to experience the prototype first hand. The curriculum was generated from themes of interest and issues of importance. It did not come from standard textbooks with predetermined learning objectives. It was experiential learning at its finest.

Kino Learning Center

I need to describe the two alternative schools I helped established. The abuse I encountered in my formative years greatly influenced the development of these programs. While they fit the progressive education model, they were also manifestations of my personal, silent protest against the abuse experienced by children, teens and young adults as they struggled to find their place in the world, just as I had.

I knew instinctively the traditional school model did not honor the young people it was designed to serve. The inherent structure of traditional schools, whether public, private or Catholic, is designed to keep kids under control. If I was going to commit my professional life to the field of alternative education, I was determined—perhaps even destined—to create a school that was warm, inviting, creative, radical and effective.

I replaced my philosophy and theology mentors with radical educational scholars: John Dewey, Johann Pestalozzi, Maria Montessori, Jerome Bruner, Herb Kohl, George Dennison, Joe Featherstone, A.S. Neill, Ted Sizer, Alfie Kohn and Jonathan Kozol. I had the privilege of getting to know some of them personally over the years.

My mom supported my commitment to read and research every book and document on the progressive education movement. Her generosity allowed me to visit many schools in the United States and England that put into action the theories described in progressive education literature. After visiting several schools that merely paid lip service to radical educational reform, I called my mom and confessed that her continued investment might be a waste of money.

She said, "Keep searching for great schools, but remember, it's also important to know what NOT to do." She was absolutely correct. I could see what was wrong with the alternative schools I visited. Even better, I could envision how to improve them.

I only saw one school that truly pushed my values and perceptions about education. Again, it was my mom who made it possible for me to visit A.S. Neill's Summerhill School, a co-educational boarding school in Suffolk, England. Founded in 1921, Summerhill is the original, alternative "free school." Despite nearly a century of criticism, it continues to be an influential model for progressive, democratic education around the world. Imagine a school where kids have the freedom to be themselves, and where students define their own success. Where the entire school community deals collectively with issues, and each person has an equal right to be heard. Where you can play all day if you want, where there is time and space to sit and dream. This is the spirit that drives the Summerhill School program.

For twenty-six years (1965–1991), I had the honor of assisting teachers, students and parents in planning and developing Kino Learning Center, Inc. in Tucson, Arizona, believed to be the only K-12, alternative Catholic school in the United States. With the assistance of extremely generous backers, Dennis and Susan DeConcini and Burt and Nancy Kinerk, we built a one-room schoolhouse on ten acres of magnificent desert land north of Tucson. There were gardens, animal centers, nature paths and a cabin in the Catalina Mountains for overnight retreats. The amazing teachers reached deep within themselves in order to have children and teens extend and connect with the world around them. We provided a hands-on learning environment where children between the ages of six and eighteen viewed themselves as partners in learning with compassionate, capable teachers.

As Kino teachers, we lived our values, even if doing so required that we question and confront our own beliefs. We were intensely committed to the love of learning and a sense of community.

Love of Learning

The kids were the center of gravity in the school—it was all about them. We wanted children to become not only good learners but also good people. We took our cues from them while being aware of the differences among them. Since each student was unique, incorporating a single set of policies, expectations or assignments would have been counterproductive as well as disrespectful.

The curriculum wasn't just based on our interests; it was based on their interests. The teachers had broadly conceived themes and objectives, yet they didn't design courses of study *for* the students; they designed projects *with* them, and they welcomed unexpected detours. The curriculum was constantly changing and was never the same from year to year.

The students played a vital role in helping design the curriculum, formulate questions, seek out and create answers, think through possibilities and evaluate their own degree of success. Students were asked to construct their own understanding of ideas rather than passively absorb information and develop rote skills. The last thing we wanted to do was fill kids with bits of knowledge through the use of worksheets, lectures, quizzes, homework and grades. We couldn't justify grades and tests because they promoted short-term skills rather than long-term attitudes and behaviors. We eliminated homework because parents believed it was meaningless, contributed to stress within the family and detracted from quality evening time together. They were absolutely right.

We organized the day around projects, problems and questions rather than facts, skills and content separated into subjects. We tried to get kids to think deeply about issues that mattered to them. Students understood ideas and concepts and applied them to new situations and problems. This skill was the epitome of higher order thinking.

Kino Learning Center was not a touchy-feely, undemanding environment for children designed by idealistic, hippie teachers and parents. It was a well-planned environment where we all worked together to create a culture of learning and caring. Parents and teachers believed meeting the needs of children by nourishing their curiosity, creativity and commitment should take precedence over preparing them to be college scholars or qualified employees.

A Sense of Community

The Kino kids learned with and from one another in a caring community. Interdependence counted more than independence. Perhaps the most important aspect of the school took place within family-grouped homerooms where students shared their goals each morning and met for a short follow-up session each afternoon just prior to dismissal. The homerooms were unique family settings where students ages six through eighteen chose to be members of a specific group. Young children sat in the laps of older students as each shared and assessed their goals for the day. The setting simulated a close-knit family of varying aged siblings gathered around the dinner table. These family-grouped homerooms contributed greatly to the profound sense of community we were able to achieve within the school.

Competition was discouraged. It undermined cooperation and a sense of community. We replaced team sports with cooperative games and lifelong sports such as golf, swimming, tennis, dancing, aerobics, hiking and camping.

The Kino teachers believed in "working with" rather than "doing to" the students. We refrained from offering extrinsic rewards for complying with adult expectations, and readily celebrated the contributions individuals made to the community. Instead of punitive responses to misbehavior, we emphasized logical consequences that would re-establish trust and mutuality. Both children and adults were ready and willing to initiate ways to restore community.

Kino students participated in retreats on Mt. Lemmon, an hour drive up the Catalina Mountains just north of the school, to solidify community in profound ways. The school owned a magnificent cabin, and used it regularly for a variety of overnight gatherings related to increasing communication, developing character traits or introducing meditation techniques to reduce stress and increase inner peace. Activities often related to the arts or the natural environment. A favorite activity was hiking in the cool air, and then sitting together in front of a roaring fire for hot chocolate and warm conversation. We sometimes rented the Kino cabin to other non-profit groups for a nominal fee used to support our retreats and maintain the facility.

While Kino Learning Center was appealing to students, it was also productive for them. Solid research supports the fact that, when students are invited to help direct their own learning and are able to spend time thinking about ideas rather than memorizing facts and practicing skills, they not only enjoy what they're doing, they do it better. Our graduates were and continue to be the best measurement of our success. Well into adulthood, with some approaching middle age, they remain excited about learning. They see learning as synonymous with life! That is our ultimate goal. The school rose to national prominence as we served kids with competence and compassion. We hosted thousands of visitors per year, as dedicated teachers hungered to see and experience educational ecstasy in action.

Several Kino teachers became national speakers on alternative education, myself included. I received one thousand dollars per "slide show." The largest group I ever addressed was eight thousand people. My fee for that group came to twelve and a half cents per person. We established a fund that my brother Jim referred to as our "play dough." This revenue allowed the students to take fabulous extended field trips to National Parks and beyond. In an effort to assure equality among students, we did not ask parents to pay for these expeditions.

✿

Kino teachers published over thirty activity books gleaned from our on-going, original curriculum. One series of values books became bestsellers, with over two million copies sold nationally. For their extra effort, the Kino teachers were given a small stipend and a share in the royalties. The remaining royalties, which totaled about one hundred thousand dollars annually, went to the school. I transposed the aerospace curriculum I wrote and tested with our elementary and junior high students into a national curriculum supported by NASA and the Young Astronaut Council of the United States. As NASA prepared various Shuttle missions and satellite launches, the Kinonauts and I prepared parallel activities that students performed at home or in classrooms, as they watched NASA astronauts and mission control communicate via satellite and cable television.

We selected an area of the school to build a scale model of the working and living quarters aboard the Shuttle orbiter. The orbiter was equipped with a cockpit, galley, sleeping quarters, laboratory and private room with a port-a-potty. Teams of Kinonauts "launched" and lived aboard the Shuttle for extended periods of time—from one to five days—as they communicated with students in charge of mission control outside the spacecraft. The Kinonauts and mission control facilitators participated in ongoing, simulated flight scenarios, as adults watched their progress on video screens from a distance.

This project was instrumental to my selection as Arizona's representative for the Teacher-in-Space Program. I continued to write the Young Astronaut Council aerospace curriculum for ten years. The learning packets were translated into five languages (Japanese, Russian, Chinese, French and German) for world distribution. This venture added significant "play dough" for Kino teachers and students to develop creative learning projects. NASA gave the Kino kids special clearance into Edwards Air Force Base in southern California to watch numerous shuttle landings as astronauts returned to Earth.

Another memorable field trip included a journey to Scammon's Lagoon in Mexico's Baja peninsula to watch gray whales birthing their calves. The teachers and students made the long trip by van. I managed to secure the assistance of a pilot with a small plane to fly me and another Sister from Tucson to Baja. I told the teachers that, if we circled their campsite along the beach, they should bring the kids to meet us at a dirt landing strip a few miles away. They did not know I had secured permission from the parents to allow the kids to take plane rides over the area to observe the whale migration and birthing process. We ate a leisurely, delicious meal at a nearby restaurant as we waited for the teachers and students to take off with excitement and descend with profound reverence for whales and their habitat. As we camped that evening with the teachers and students, I did not want to sleep. It was the only night of my life where I could listen to whales spouting in my front yard.

To show how one learning experience may lead to another, students and teachers on the Baja whale-watching trip began another incredible activity. They decided to complete the rigorous work of obtaining their SCUBA diving certification, culminating in demonstration of their skills off the coast in San Carlos, Mexico, the second best diving spot in the world after the Great Barrier Reef off of Australia.

Other teachers and I took the classes along with the kids and became certified with them in open-water, deep water and night diving techniques. At the time, I was recovering from cancer radiation treatment and only had the energy to sink about forty to fifty feet to the ocean floor and watch the group.

There, in the silence of the sea, I had my most incredible experience as a teacher. I watched as a young student "danced" with a sea lion. The "couple" introduced themselves with a nose-to-nose greeting, their bodies parallel to the ocean floor. The sea lion took the lead by encircling the child then returning to the "nose position." The child followed the lead as he mimicked the animal. The sea lion backed up as the child swam forward. Then the child backed up as the sea lion moved forward. They mimicked each others movements for quite awhile, then after a final nose-to-nose greeting, the sea lion turned away and joined his peers, while the student did the same.

I was glad I had learned the technique of clearing my mask underwater. This time, however, it was not filled with seawater. Rather, my mask and eyes were filled with joy and ecstasy of the moment. If my radiation treatment had only gotten me as far as that moment in time, the effort would have been worth it!

You might ask: If progressive education is so terrific, why have so few schools and school districts implemented this model? That's simple: While progressive schools don't require more money to operate, they take a lot more commitment, planning and work on the part of the students, teachers and parents. Kino Learning Center asked a lot of its participants because it required real thinking. Teachers had to help students *make sense* out of a topic rather than merely memorize information and facts about it. Teachers also had to know a lot about pedagogy because no amount of knowledge related to content can make teachers true facilitators of learning. The Kino teachers are also comfortable with uncertainty. They abandoned predictable "right answers," encouraging students to play an active role in the quest for meaning. Above all, Kino Learning Center required from everyone involved an incredibly high level of trust. Teachers were willing to give up control and let students take significant ownership of their learning and lives. Parents trusted teachers and kids to work together to make sense of their learning and communicate its results in new, unfamiliar ways using models, demonstrations, exhibits, presentations and artistic and literary pieces. For the Kino community, the risks seemed reasonable since there is not one shred of evidence offered by traditional schools to show that standardized tests, homework or conventional discipline based on punishment and rewards contributed to the success of adults in work or life.

The teachers and students at Kino Learning Center lived the dream. I should have viewed it as such. Rather, I felt the stress of raising money for the future without enjoying the excitement and successes of the present moment. In looking back, I realize the Kino experience *in its entirety* was my honor and privilege. It was the happiest and most creative time of my life.

Along the way, I acquired master's degrees in biology and ecology at the University of Arizona, and a doctorate in educational leadership and curriculum development from the University of San Francisco. I studied ecology, astronomy and cosmology, as I do today, for the pure joy of escaping into nature and propelling myself to a greater understanding of the world.

The Sanctuary Movement

In the early 1980s, I became active in the Sanctuary Movement, a religious and political campaign providing a safe haven for refugees fleeing civil conflict in Central America. The Movement opposed strict federal immigration policies that made obtaining asylum difficult for Central Americans. The roots of the Sanctuary Movement may be traced to an ancient Judaic tradition in the Hebrew Bible. God commanded Moses to set aside cities of refuge (Num. 35: 9-15) where a person who committed involuntary manslaughter could go for protection from relatives of the dead, who might seek retaliation.

Most Central American refugees were fleeing political repression and violence caused by civil wars in Guatemala and El Salvador, though many also fled the Sandinistas in Nicaragua after its 1979 Revolution. In Guatemala, government-backed paramilitary groups destroyed six hundred villages, killing fifty thousand people; one hundred thousand more were never found. By 1980, the Salvadorian military death squad had killed over ten thousand people, including Archbishop Oscar Romero, three U.S. nuns (Maura Clarke, Ita Ford and Dorothy Kazel) and their lay missionary companion (Jean Donovan). I personally knew Sister Ita Ford and Jean Donovan. They were remarkable women and news of their deaths shook me to my core.

The Sanctuary Movement was born along the Arizona—Mexico border. Expatriates on their way to Tucson would travel by foot to Nogales,

Sonora. The border with Mexico runs right through the continuous metro area of Nogales, Sonora and Nogales, Arizona. The refugees met at El Santuario de Nuestra Señora Guadalupe (Sanctuary of Our Lady of Guadalupe) Catholic Church on the Mexican side. With the help of Father Ramón Quiñones, pastor of Guadalupe, immigrants travelled across the border to Sacred Heart Catholic Church in the U.S. There they were given shelter, food, legal advice and sometimes a little money. The two churches were in constant contact. Volunteers traveled frequently between the two parishes. Everyone looked the same; nobody carried passports. The refugees were then driven from Sacred Heart Church in Nogales, AZ to Southside Presbyterian Church in Tucson. By coincidence, Sacred Heart in Nogales was the parish of Mother Gerald Barry, the head of the Adrian Dominicans when I entered the convent in 1960.

On March 24, 1982, the second anniversary of Archbishop Oscar Romero's assassination, Reverend John Fife, Pastor of the Southside Presbyterian Church in Tucson, declared his church a public sanctuary. Outside the church John posted a sign that read: "This is a sanctuary for the oppressed of Central America." By 1985, Sanctuary became a national movement with roughly five hundred member-sites across the United States, including strongholds throughout Arizona, Texas and California, and in cities like Chicago and Philadelphia. Between 1980 and 1991, nearly one million Central Americans gained political asylum in the U.S.

I was privileged to help about twenty-five hundred of these people gain freedom. An unusual gift from my very conservative father proved to be a fortuitous contribution to the Sanctuary Movement in Arizona. My dad called and said the lifelong accountant at Babe's Restaurant, Mary Lynch, had died. He had given Mary a maroon, four-door Oldsmobile Cutlass. She told my dad to pass it on to me. As I drove the car from Des Moines to Tucson, I knew exactly what I would do with it. According to Arizona law, the owner of the vehicle was legally responsible if caught smuggling refugees. It was a perfect situation. Mary Lynch was responsible. After adorning her expensive car with Reagan bumper stickers, we were ready to roll, and roll we did. Every night, that car traveled back and forth from Tucson to Nogales, Sonora and Nogales, Arizona. I estimate we made at least five hundred trips before being stopped.

We lost the car but it was never traced to me.

I had a difficult time as an activist in the Sanctuary Movement while also serving as director of Kino Learning Center. It was exhausting. I worked all day and all night. My close friends cautioned me that my arrest would ruin the school. I believe everyone associated with Kino Learning Center knew what I was doing. The teachers backed me and the cause. We taught the children of refugees in the school, while families waited to be transported to Chicago and Philadelphia. Several Kino parents were active in the movement. I worried most about jeopardizing my relationship with Dennis and Susan DeConcini and Burt and Nancy Kinerk. I never discussed my moonlighting job with them, but I sensed they knew. Dennis was Pima County Attorney and Burt was a prominent Tucson lawyer. Surely they knew, but some things were best not discussed.

Trouble a World Away

The Tiananmen Square protests of 1989 were a series of mass gatherings and student-run demonstrations in and near Tiananmen Square in Beijing, in the People's Republic of China. Protesters sought political and economic reform. The liberty they most desired was freedom of the press. The People's Liberation Army of the Chinese government moved through the streets of Beijing and into Tiananmen Square, using live bullets to clear the area of protesters. The exact number of civilian deaths is not known, but estimates range from several hundred to thousands. There was worldwide condemnation of China's use of force against its people.

Upon hearing of this tragedy, I felt the need to take a stand on behalf of those killed in Tiananmen Square. A friend and I traveled to Hong Kong, where we met in secret with local Christian missionaries. We received instructions on how to smuggle Bibles into mainland China. In the interest of protecting the people and organizations involved, I won't give details about this process. We were shown how to roll Bibles and cover them with foil to resemble metal canisters when x-rayed. We packed flat books between layers of metal hangers overlapping them in ways that made the Bibles difficult to detect in our suitcases. We wore full body aprons beneath our clothing, with dozens of pockets that were stuffed with Bibles. I probably carried one hundred Bibles with me.

We traveled by train to the border of mainland China, and upon arriving we walked the contraband through tight security operated by the Chinese army. This was probably the scariest moment of my life. There I stood, covered in Bibles, staring at armed soldiers in the People's Liberation Army. When it was my turn to have my suitcases searched and x-rayed, the soldier at customs turned his back to me. I walked quickly through security without being checked. Another soldier saw what had happened. As he approached, I nervously handed him my passport. As he reached for it, the passport fell to the floor. I knew if I picked it up, he would see the Bibles in the pockets against my back. He picked up the passport without looking at it and whispered, "Come." I followed him out the back door. He pointed to a hotel about a block away and said, "Go." As I waited outside customs for the rest of the group, he again pleaded, "Go. Go." So I went.

I met the others at the hotel. We deposited the Bibles in lockers. In a day or two, thousands of Bibles would be transported by truck to people in remote villages in the Himalaya Mountains. We returned to Hong Kong by train. To this day, I believe that young soldier knew exactly what I was doing. Perhaps the one who turned his back on me in the x-ray line also knew. Either they didn't want to deal with the situation, or they, too, were Christians. I will never know.

When I later inquired about the Bibles, I was told the man driving the truck into the highlands was stopped, searched, shot and killed. For me, there aren't enough Bibles in print to equal the value of a single human life. It was then I realized the potential consequences of my acts of civil disobedience. I began to pull back, not from personal fear, but out of concern for the physical welfare of those who participated with me, especially those who followed my example and leadership.

The experience of smuggling Bibles into mainland China profoundly influenced my future actions regarding the smuggling of undocumented Mexicans into the U.S. The stress I experienced in making strides towards social justice and educational reform for myself and others came at a huge price. As Kino Learning Center grew stronger, I became weaker. I was again diagnosed with cancer, this time a more aggressive variety. I quickly lost one breast, and though I fought for a year to save my other breast, the cancer would take that one as well.

A few years later, I was diagnosed with stage-four uterine cancer. After six weeks of daily radiation treatment my doctor informed me that a mistake had been made.

He said, "Due to a computer software glitch, you received three times the intended amount of daily radiation!" I was devastated, and lost fifty pounds in the next five months, but I rarely missed a day of work.

One day in early September 1991, my world, and all I had attempted to build, came crashing down. A six-year-old child had been kidnapped from the school, and was found wandering naked in the desert several miles away. Investigators informed us she was the first child in Arizona's history to be found alive and free of sexual assault. She had been buried alive from her neck down. Her virginity had been preserved intentionally. Apparently, she was to be sacrificed that night as part of a satanic ritual, as evidenced by an altar of rocks found at the burial site.

I lost my job over the Kino kidnapping. While it was devastating, it was also necessary. For insurance purposes, the Kino Board of Directors needed to look proactive by blaming the tragedy on my educational philosophy and methodology. At the same time, I knew I could no longer trust my vision of providing alternative education programs for kids. I had created a subculture for children that protected their innocence while they enjoyed learning and delighted in life. For two decades, we lived in a bubble community while failing to consider the reality of outside threats and violence. After the kidnapping, life was never the same for the Kino Learning Center community. I allowed anger and depression to abduct my emotional and physical health. While anger dissipated eventually, legitimate sorrow has remained forever. To this day, I do not think I have recovered fully. What matters is Kino Learning Center has a happy ending. While my time there has long since ended, the school still offers a modified version of the original model I helped build. After forty years, some of the founding teachers are still working at the school.

After my time with Kino Learning Center, I put my degrees to work at the University of Arizona where I founded Science-To-Go, a mobile outreach program for children and teens throughout Tucson and Southern Arizona. After raising significant funds for elementary and high school science students to interact with the University of Arizona, I was told to fudge data to show money being spent in ways it was not. I was told to sign false financial reports. When I refused, it was suggested that my moral principles may be too high for higher education. Before I quit, I sued the University of Arizona and received a significant amount of money—enough to launch my next dream. As I entered the sunset of my life, I knew I had morphed into a very angry human being. I vowed never to be hurt again. I camouflaged my rage to resemble intensity, commitment and passion, but underneath it all I was filled with anger that bordered on rage.

César Chávez Learning Community, Inc.

April 20, 1999 marks the day of the Columbine High School killings near Littleton, Colorado. Two seniors slaughtered twelve students and a teacher and injured twenty-one other students. An additional three people were injured while attempting to escape. The pair of students responsible then committed suicide.

On the day of the Columbine massacre, I vowed once more to establish an alternative learning environment for children and teenagers. I envisioned a public charter school for Mexican-American and Native American kids in South Tucson. Arizona's Department of Education would supply sufficient monthly revenue to operate this alternative charter school. As a public school, we would be able to compete for additional federal and state funding for support programs. I was excited about returning "home" to the *barrio*.

Arizona had developed the finest charter school system in the United States. The template was cutting edge; outrageously creative. Whoever dreamed it into existence was a genius. It truly put power in the hands of teachers and parents at the local level. We had the freedom to implement our vision, and were limited only by the parameters of our own imaginations.

I worked with teachers, students and parents to birth César Chávez Learning Community, Inc.—an alternative charter middle and high school for the economically poor yet culturally rich families in South Tucson. Children ages eleven through thirteen attended César Chávez Middle School and those ages fourteen through eighteen attended Aztlán Academy. The name of the middle school was controversial because it honored César Chávez, an American farm worker, labor leader and civil rights activist who, with Dolores Huerta, co-founded the National Farm Workers Association, which later became the United Farm Workers (UFW). César Estrada Chávez (1927–93), born in Yuma, Arizona, became a well-known known Latino civil rights activist and was strongly supported by the American Labor Movement, which was eager to enroll Latino members. His public relations approach to unionism and aggressive-but-nonviolent tactics transformed the farm workers' struggle in southern California to a nationwide support system. César Chávez and Dolores Huerta became major historical icons for the Latino community, symbolizing support for migrant farm workers with their slogan: *¡Sí se puede!* (Yes we can!).

I met César Chávez in the early days of the Sanctuary Movement. He was passing through Tucson with one hundred migrant workers from Delano, California on their way to a protest in Michigan. It was my job to find one hundred mattresses, pillows, blankets, etc. for the group, since they were staying at the school overnight. Later, after César died, I got to know Dolores Huerta and her husband, Richard Chávez (César's brother), who came to Tucson periodically to attend meetings and marches. Dolores and Richard became friends and supporters of our school community.

The name of the high school, Aztlán Academy, was seen as offensive to the misguided, tea-sipping conservatives who insisted that Arizona and the American Southwest had always belonged to them. The high school was named Aztlán Academy to remind the students that the land on which they live is their ancestral home. Aztlán is the home of the Nahua people, one of the main cultural groups in Mexico. It is also the homeland of the Aztec people. (*Aztec* is the Nahuatl word for *people from Aztlán.*)

César Chávez Middle School and Aztlán Academy operated together in developing a strong sense of community both within and between the two schools. We had been extremely successful with "family grouping" at Kino Learning Center, despite a twelve year age difference among students. A seven year variance among middle and high school students was an achievable goal. As with Kino Learning Center during the Sanctuary Movement, we did not attempt to identify undocumented students from Mexico who might be staying with families, relatives and friends in Tucson.

It became apparent to me that the kids in South Tucson were very angry people. As they were never shown how to acquire positive identities, they claimed the streets as a means of establishing their individuality. Gangs, weapons, violence, drugs and reckless sex disguised themselves as opportunities for excitement and gave the kids a false sense of empowerment. I was determined to hire teachers who came from the same communities as our students, teachers who would be absolutely committed to seeing that the kids—their kids—enjoyed life and succeeded within it. I made sure the teachers did everything they could to fill the massive gaps between the ages of the students and their academic skill levels. Almost every student who attended César Chávez on a regular basis advanced two years academically for each year spent in school. Some progressed far more quickly, improving three to five years in reading and writing in a single school year. This was an amazing feat, since the majority of our kids—ages eleven through eighteen—came to us reading, writing and computing at first, second and third grade levels. Poor kids, given the opportunity to learn, are as smart as any other kids. They do not lack ability; they merely lack opportunity. It was our job to make sure that opportunity knocked, even on the doors of illegally occupied homes, automobiles and neighborhood shelters where many of our students lived.

The kids soon realized that Broadway Boulevard, which divides Tucson north and south, wasn't all that broad. To the north was an exciting world for them to explore. Sixty miles south, just beyond the U.S.-Mexico border, was their motherland, where ancient and recent ancestors bequeathed to them a culture rich in tradition and ritual. The teachers at César Chávez Middle School and Aztlán Academy had a profound understanding of our mission: to create an alternative learning environment driven by the goals, values and traditions of the Mexican-American families we served.

The kids had daily access to a farm where they integrated science with animal husbandry. Our Mariachi group performed locally and nationally. There were numerous opportunities for team as well as individual sports, and ongoing activities that emphasized proper nutrition and physical fitness. In an effort to create a deep sense of community, the students participated in desert and mountain retreats, where they learned to forgive and love through communication and community.

We took the kids on extended field trips throughout the U.S. and Mexico. They swam in the ocean, watched whales, camped at the bottom of the Grand Canyon, visited numerous National Parks and survived in the Alaskan wilderness. Wherever I was asked to speak, I insisted the kids help give the presentation. Organizations paid to bring me and the kids from Tucson's barrio all over the United States: New York, Washington, D. C., Chicago, Seattle, Orlando, Honolulu, and numerous cities throughout southern California. It felt like I was back in my stride, like the dream that had been "kidnapped" from Kino Learning Center might still be achievable.

No Child Left Behind

The No Child Left Behind Act (NCLB) was initiated by George W. Bush and signed into law on January 2, 2002. The NCLB Act supported standards-based education rather than our project-based model, which was approved by the Arizona State Department of Education. Standards-based education was founded on the premise that setting high standards and establishing measurable goals would improve individual outcomes in education. Since our state-run school received federal funding, we were required to administer the AIMS test: Arizona's Instrument to Measure Standards.

At that time, the most common way for a student to graduate from an Arizona public high school was to pass the writing, reading and mathematics content areas of the AIMS test. Basically, what a student accomplished in class during his/her four years had no bearing on graduation. A student who got reasonably good grades all through high school and failed one area of the AIMS test could be denied a high school diploma.

The NCLB Act was the beginning of the end for César Chávez Learning Community. Prior to NCLB, the Arizona State Board of Charter Schools fully supported our progressive educational model. However, after NCLB, we could no longer continue with our state-approved program. Now it was all about passing the AIMS test. We were forced to teach every State Standard to every student in every grade every school year. We were "free" to continue our alternative school model within the parameters of State Standards and mandatory national testing. Our once-personalized curriculum was now driven by Arizona State Standards. Like everyone else, we were now teaching to the test.

Despite having enrolled at César Chávez with elementary-level skills, many of our high school seniors actually passed the reading and writing portions of the AIMS test. Eventually, the Arizona State Charter School Board allowed us to augment student math scores because of good grades received in high school math classes. However, the new system proved a great impediment to what we were trying to achieve with our students in terms of personal development. The fundamental reason the César Chávez teachers opposed the NCLB Act was because it robbed us of our identity, creativity and independence. Our philosophy and methodology were no longer acceptable to the Arizona Department of Education. We were viewed as inherently subversive.

The person in power, the Executive Director of the Arizona State Board of Charter Schools, was committed to closing César Chávez Learning Community, and made a point of telling us repeatedly and publicly. In her view, the school was not designed to have a long, stable life. It was too radical; too controversial. My friends warned me to slow down and be discreet. But I was too angry and frustrated to sacrifice my personal values and professional principles in a losing effort to be politically correct. I was unapologetically committed to being educationally correct, even though I knew I was politically incorrect. I had been a passionate defender of the progressive education movement for forty years and a recent supporter of the charter school movement. Unfortunately, I had now become an outspoken critic of the No Child Left Behind Act. I am certain this contributed significantly to the closure of César Chávez Learning Community in May 2010.

The students of César Chávez Learning Community should never have been forced to take standardized tests. We received alternative school status within the charter school division, which allowed us to choose assessments and approach learning in unconventional ways. We wanted every student to graduate with skills to get better than dead-end, minimum wage jobs or be successful at the local community college. In fact, we had dozens of graduates who volunteered to attend César Chávez Learning Community for a fifth year for the opportunity to be transported to and from the local community college. They were to have free access to our computer lab and receive free tutoring for their college classes from their former high school teachers. The Arizona State Board of Charter Schools wanted nothing to do with our plan for success. They said, "Your kids should be able to make it through college like everybody else."

Today's progressive education model is in direct opposition to the traditional nineteenth-century education model, which was intended to prepare students for college. Furthermore, traditional education is strongly differentiated by socioeconomic levels. Simply stated, rich kids are better prepared to succeed in college than poor kids. Most of the poor kids I know do not have parents who speak English fluently. They were not read to as children. They do not have private bedrooms or their own desks that hold personal treasures and learning supplies. They do not have laptops, video game consoles, smart phones, tablets or reliable access to the Internet. Most poor kids do not have private tutors to keep them ahead in school. They do not take lessons in music, art, dance, swimming, gymnastics, etc. They do not visit college campuses as juniors in high school.

Life's educational opportunities are not distributed equally and they never will be. It was inconceivable to me that two freshmen in high school, one at a ninth grade level and one at a third grade level, would be at the same place academically by the time they are seniors. I am not implying that rich kids are smarter than poor kids; rather I am saying that rich kids have more advantages in life than poor kids. Poor kids, simply put, are not equal-opportunity learners.

The more I defended the unique programs offered by César Chávez Learning Community, intended to assist American citizens as well as undocumented residents of South Tucson, the more I realized the Executive Director of the Arizona State Board of Charter Schools had pinned a target on my back. No radical, outspoken nun with a doctorate in educational administration and curriculum development was going to run a controversial public school for poor kids, no matter how happy they were or how much they excelled. Unfortunately, every teacher in the school was clearly under attack as well. The Executive Director was out to get us and warned, in her own words, "I have never lost an argument." She criticized everything we did. I had forgotten the important lesson my mom taught me: Never get into a power struggle with the person who has all the power.

I taught two science classes for sixth through eighth graders. The Executive Director of the State Charter School Board insisted I teach three separate lessons at three separate grade levels for full periods each day. Instead, I taught the entire group the eighth grade science curriculum and declared the sixth and seventh graders to be "honor students." I won that battle. She insisted that teacher aides, trained and certified to teach an amazingly successful reading program, were not qualified to teach a Language Arts class. We gave these kids a separate Language Arts class and offered the reading class as an elective course. We won that battle. The teachers were told that homeroom time could not be counted as legitimate class instruction. We submitted a national curriculum that allowed us to teach character education as a legitimate course. We won that argument. The teachers were told that any time spent tutoring would not count as legitimate class time. We lost this battle badly. Class time was often spent trying to fill the gap between the kids' ability and their grade levels. When fourteen through eighteen year olds entered high school on a first through third grade level in reading, writing and math, there were hours, if not years, of remedial learning.

We were told we could teach anything we wanted, as long as all the standards in every subject for each grade were covered each year. I wondered how much time would be left to pursue what really interested the kids and teachers. While we grudgingly implemented the State's educational standards and testing, students repeatedly failed to pass the math portion of the AIMS test. The No Child Left Behind Act gave the Arizona State Board of Charter Schools permission to eliminate us. Yet, the longer I kept the situation in litigation, the more time the teachers had to transform the lives of the kids who needed them.

The last five years of the school's short eleven year history was a bitter battle of survival. Eventually we succumbed to the pressures of the Executive Director. Our amazing teachers moved to the unemployment line while our resilient kids, once labeled "at risk" of dropping out of school, fulfilled that prophecy by returning to the streets from which they came.

The No Child Left Behind Act missed its mark. I can show you a few hundred kids who were "left behind" and a few thousand more we could have helped. Most poor kids, due to the lack of opportunities available to them, are left behind. It's just a matter of how far. In spite of their skill limitations, most of our kids progressed adequately from one year to the next. Every kid who made the effort to come to school on a regular basis eventually graduated. Many kids who enrolled with us were initially unable to read, but graduated on the twelfth grade level. However, some who stayed the entire four years could only read at the ninth grade level. We graduated them as well. That was our crime.

I imagine the Executive Director of the Arizona State Board of Charter Schools would say: "The César Chávez teachers and students got what they deserved because they simply did not measure up." I might ask her in response: "Why do we use State Standards and tests to measure the academic ability of rich kids who have greater access to opportunity, resources and life experiences against poor kids who have less access to these same benefits?" The system clearly lacks justice!

Nothing is equal on the continuum of life when money and opportunity are unevenly distributed among participants. When the Arizona Charter School Board denied our students and teachers their Mexican-American identity, we had no recourse but to "drop out" as a matter of integrity. After fighting the system for eleven years, César Chávez Learning Community closed on June 30, 2010.

After the school closed, most of the middle school students and younger high school students enrolled in traditional public and charter schools. Many of the older high school students opted to return to the streets rather than attempt to be successful in the traditional schools they'd left years ago. Only three of the twenty teachers remained in teaching. The others, myself included, could not see ourselves teaching within traditional learning models that neither made sense nor aided the disadvantaged families we served.

¡Sí se Puede! (Yes We Can!)

During the 1980s, over a million combined Mexicans and Central Americans poured into the United States, fleeing life-threatening repression and human rights violations by their governments. At the time, federal immigration policies denied the majority of these people political asylum because their governments were allies of the U.S.

For many years, Americans and Mexicans were free to cross the border in either direction without a passport. However, the bombing of the World Trade Center and Pentagon on September 11, 2001 and the national security laws enacted as a result slammed our borders shut. Today, Mexicans are considered economic migrants fleeing poverty, not refugees fleeing governmental repression. Little regard is given to the fact that poverty and repression go hand in hand. As Mexico supports the Free Trade Agreement, United States, European, and Asian factory owners exploit hundreds of thousands of workers in *maquiladoras* (assembly plants) along the United States-Mexico border. Seeking to escape this exploitation, many Mexicans and Central Americans migrate to the United States, where they are confronted with racism and more repression.

H.R. 4437 redefined illegal immigrants as felons and punished anyone guilty of providing them assistance. The bill imposed an incredible five-year mandatory minimum prison sentence on humanitarian workers, public-school teachers, church volunteers and others who assisted anyone who later turned out to be in the U.S. without proper legal documentation. It also called for the construction of a border security fence along the 2,000-mile United States-Mexico border.

H.R. 4437 was passed by the United States House of Representatives on December 16, 2005 by a vote of two hundred and thirty-nine to one hundred and eighty-two, with ninety-two percent of Republicans supporting and eighty-two percent of Democrats opposing, but did not pass the Senate. The bill was the first piece of legislation passed by a House of Congress in the United States relative to the illegal immigration debate, and served as the catalyst for the 2006 U.S. immigration reform protests. In March of 2006 Cardinal Roger Mahony, Archbishop of Los Angeles, the largest U.S. diocese, instructed the priests and nuns to disregard The Border Protection, Anti-terrorism, and Illegal Immigration Control Act of 2005 (H.R. 4437), which criminalized providing humanitarian aid to persons without first checking their legal status, in effect forcing priests, ministers, rabbis and volunteers to become quasi-immigration enforcement officials.

On May 1, 2006, The Great American Boycott in support of immigration rights arose from protests against H.R. 4437. It was initiated by a small band of grassroots advocates in Los Angeles, inspired in part by the United Farm Workers Movement led by César Chávez in the 1960s. Throngs of immigrants and advocates took to the streets of major U.S. cities to protest immigration laws. Kids skipped school. Men and women walked off their jobs. Others didn't bother going to work. Families abstained from buying anything. Businesses shut down for lack of patrons or employees. The intent of The Great American Boycott was to demonstrate, through direct action, the extent to which labor provided by immigrants contributed to the U.S. economy.

Supporters rallied for general amnesty and legalization programs for non-citizens. The event included millions of participants across the nation. Crowds in Los Angeles were estimated at six hundred thousand. In Chicago, an estimated four hundred thousand people participated. The students, teachers and parents who made up the César Chávez Learning Community were fully involved in the Great American Boycott. The majority of our students and teachers marched in Tucson, while we sent smaller delegations to participate in Phoenix and Los Angeles. I marched with our kids in Phoenix along with ten thousand other people.

Our school, located just a few blocks from Rev. John Fife's Southside Presbyterian Church, continued to support people seeking sanctuary and desiring to immigrate to the U.S., regardless of their reasons. We supported children whom we had known for years, whose undocumented parents used fake social security numbers to work, pay mortgages and car loans, declare income and pay taxes in the U.S.

As our students and family members were deported, I once more took up the task of assisting them in reentering the country—their country. I cannot describe how this is done, again for the safety of those involved. I will say, however, that the procedure required to smuggle immigrants across the Mexican border into the U.S. is far more difficult and dangerous today than in previous decades.

I am acutely aware of the risks people take, as well as the penalties they endure, to seek refuge in this country in an effort to secure political freedom and financial security for themselves and their families. Indeed, I find striking similarities between the smuggling of immigrants into the United States and Bibles into the People's Republic of China. Both activities were supported by people who believed they had not only the right, but the moral obligation to give people access to opportunities they would otherwise never be allowed.

When facilitating the transport of undocumented people into the U.S., I feared the potential consequences of my actions would fall upon the people I served. The only thing that prevented me from further participation was the likelihood that someday a U.S. Border Patrol agent would shoot and kill a student or family member because of my lack of savvy and experience. I honestly do not think I could live with such an outcome. I am still haunted by the spirit of that young Chinese man who gave his life so his compatriots could read the Bible. In my dreams I ask him, "Was it worth it?"

While the Arizona Department of Education sent letters instructing schools to refrain from participating in protests supporting Mexicans seeking American citizenship, we sent letters to parents asking that they allow the kids to stand with pride and march with purpose. Not only did we march, we organized and energized rallies throughout Tucson, Phoenix and Los Angeles. We chanted *¡Sí se Puede!* years before anyone chanted it the night we elected President Obama. We carried flags showing our solidarity with America, Mexico and the United Farm Workers, all emblazoned with a black eagle on a red background. We rekindled the fire in the hearts of our *nanas* and *tatas*—our grandparents, who lived in dire poverty as migrant workers on nearby farms not long ago.

In April of 2006, a large demonstration related to the Great American Boycott began at our school, culminating at the Evo DeConcini Federal Courthouse in downtown Tucson. Evo DeConcini served as Attorney General of Arizona from 1948 to 1949, and a Justice of the Arizona Supreme Court from 1949 to 1953. Evo and his wife Ora were strong supporters of Kino Learning Center. I considered them personal friends.

At the time, all Tucson public schools were in lockdown. No students or teachers were allowed to participate in the demonstration yet César Chávez Learning Community believed it was our civil and moral duty to participate in this human rights rally. As we marched by Tucson High School, many Mexican-American students lined the windows and cheered us on. Our kids motioned for them to join us. I watched as throngs of Tucson High kids ran out of class, jumped the locked fence and joined us on the march.

We were not permitted to enter the federal building, and were told to conduct the protest from across the street in front of "Evo's place." The courthouse is a prominent building in downtown Tucson. It has massive front windows on each floor of the building. A few students from Tucson High asked if I would take their Mexican flag into the building, go to the top floor and hold the flag at the window so they could see it from the street. Before I could answer, "Yes," they handed me their only Mexican flag. I knew I could not let them down.

As I entered the courthouse a guard yelled, "Stop! You can't enter this building."

I said, "I have an appointment with my lawyer."

He said, "Who is your lawyer?"

I fired back, "Evo DeConcini." I kept walking to the elevator, where a guard of Mexican-American descent sat at a table.

I whispered, "Sir. I am Sister Judy Bisignano. I am an Adrian Dominican nun. I have a favor to ask you."

He said, "I know who you are. Thank you for helping my people."

I said, "Sir, I have a Mexican flag and the kids want me to take it to the window on the top floor and hold it up for them for a few seconds. I knew Evo DeConcini personally and I think Evo would want me to do this."

He said, "I knew the Judge, too, and I don't think he would want you to do that."

I said, "Please, Sir, I just want to give these kids a little hope. Evo would want that."

The guard looked at me carefully, and said, "Use this service elevator. I'm going on break. You must have slipped through then. You have five minutes."

I went to the top floor and proceeded to the window. There was a huge mass of people. I had no idea how large the crowd had grown. I unfurled the large, silk Mexican flag and held it to the window. I could hear protesters screaming their approval. After displaying the flag for a few minutes, I gave the kids the protest sign: my right arm bent but extended over my head with my fist closed. I gathered the flag and proceeded down the service elevator.

As I passed the guard I said, "Evo and I thank you, sir."

As I rejoined the protesters, the kids were shouting, "Snow Cone! Snow Cone!" I returned the flag to the kids from Tucson High and asked, "Why are we chanting Snow Cone?" They said, "It's for you. Your hair—you look like a snow cone! We are thanking you." I guess this white-haired old nun had put on a little weight. They now call me Snow Cone when they used to call me Q-Tip.

Save Saturdays for the Real Basics

The best way we could teach important life skills to our girls was to hold Saturday Girls' Club, sponsored by the Adrian Dominicans Sisters. My friend Sandra Morse was the César Chávez Board President, and advised the staff as a communications expert. Her mother was born in Guadalajara, Mexico, and the kids considered her "one of them."

On Saturday mornings, our female teachers would transport the girls between their homes and school. Sandra always prepared an elegant brunch. We covered the tables with bright Mexican tablecloths and adorned them with candles, fresh flowers, etc. The plates were ceramic, the silver was silver and the glasses were glass. Everything came from Sandra's kitchen. Every Saturday was a pageant.

One girl commented, "I never knew people lived like this!"

The conversations and activities that took place during the Saturday Girls' Club were simple, bold, and memorable; sometimes light-hearted; sometimes intense; always life-changing. We shared personal insights in the face of deep intimate questions. "What is my story?" "How would I describe myself using three positive words?" "What do I dream about? How can I make my dream a reality?" "If I could change one thing about myself, what would it be? Why?"

Separate, overnight retreats were held for boys and girls. We descended upon desert retreat houses and nature resorts. The kids loved every minute of these social-spiritual-eco adventures. These retreats were important, transformational events that changed the lives of the students in profound ways. Again, the student retreats were directed by Sandra Morse, assisted by teachers and sponsored by the Adrian Dominican Sisters.

It is important to describe the intensity of these retreats. Sandra would explain that sharing "your story," then moving beyond its pain with new eyes, insight and possibilities, was the purpose—the destiny—of every human being. She explained that our time together was precious. She asked the students to come to the front of the room and share their stories in deep, personal ways. She assured them that, before the end of the retreat, she would show them how to make their stories—their lives—more joyful and complete.

The stories of the students often went like this:

- My friends and I were at a party. Things got out of control. We shot into a crowd. A kid fell to the ground. He died. I wonder if my bullet was the one that killed him.

- I walked in and found my brother dead on the floor. His girlfriend said it was suicide. I don't believe her.

- I am 14 years old. I don't want this baby. I want an abortion but it costs seven hundred dollars. I don't have the money.

- I don't shoplift for beer and cigarettes. I shoplift for diapers and baby formula.

- All they did was stop and get gas. Shots were fired. My brother and *tio* (uncle) are dead. Now I have two brothers and two *tios* who have been shot to death.

- It's hard for a boy to talk about rape. Everyone thinks I should have fought back. I couldn't stop him.

- My dad threw me out of the house. I wanted to kill myself. I ran into a guy who gave me some black tar heroine and a syringe. He showed me how to use it. Another guy came along and I sold it to him for ten dollars. I ate at McDonalds and went home.

Sandra is the only person I know who could not only get the kids to talk about what had happened to them, but who could then show them the power and resolution that sharing their stories could bring. By the end of the retreat, the kids knew revisiting the trauma in their lives would be meaningless without forgiving themselves and others or without moving beyond their old stories. I watched the kids leave behind intense personal grief at the retreat, and I was learning to do the same.

My Amazon Immersion

Kino Learning Center and César Chávez Learning Community were founded on one basic principle: *I am the only one who can be responsible for me.* This belief served me well professionally for fifty years. It became the key component in my survival backpack as I ventured forward in life as an ordinary person, divested of my role of radical educator. Sandra Morse had similar tools but different language in her ideology arsenal. She would ask, "Why are you living in your old story? When are you going to rise up and claim your destiny?"

In 2009, a year before the closure of César Chávez Learning Community, Sandra Morse graciously positioned herself to catch me before I slipped deeper into my depression. She invited me to join her in visiting the Ecuadorian rainforest, where she conducts trips for the Pachamama Alliance, based in San Francisco. I didn't know it at the time, but this experience would open an entirely new vista in my search for inner peace. During the second semester of 2009, as César Chávez Learning Community was losing its fight for survival, I accompanied Sandra on one of her trips to Ecuador.

As a nun, I engaged in various collectives that confronted institutions and systems of social injustice that benefited a few and disempowered many. I was painfully aware of the disparity of class income, and institutional racism in America. Since I believe our American democratic process contributes to many of these crises, I took action on a personal, local and international level to counteract them. But, as always, my pursuits were intellectual rather than spiritual. I acted out of a religion-based institution without a spiritual-based guidance system. Religion and spirituality are not synonymous.

Sandra Morse and her husband, Michael, were active members of the Pachamama Alliance. Since 2000, the Pachamama Alliance has provided conversations and experiences that educate and inspire individuals to be proactive creators of a global future by taking a stand for a thriving, just and sustainable world.

The Pachamama Alliance represents a grassroots movement that democratizes our democracy by proposing a new planetary future, one that includes both indigenous and modern worldviews. It connects human beings with their inherent dignity by transforming human relationships between ourselves and the natural world. In the midst of this global struggle, the Pachamama Alliance does not leave people with a sense of discouragement and despair. It offers hope and inspiration in the face of urgency. It connects like-minded people, as we discuss what's meaningful and possible for the world right now. It suggests ways to heal Pachamama by becoming proactive leaders for environmental change in our local communities and the world.

The Pachamama Alliance was the perfect organization with which to align myself. Just as the Adrian Dominicans offered me a platform on which to take a public stand for social justice, the Pachamama Alliance provided a stage whereby I could speak for eco-justice. They provided an international model for shifting the trajectory of climate change on the planet.

Sandra Morse was determined that I visit the Amazon Rainforest. She recognized long before I did that if my trip was to be a life-changing, transformational experience, it would have to be a journey from my head into my heart and soul. But, as always, I prepared for my future intellectually, rather than emotionally and spiritually.

Two experiences prepared me for my upcoming jungle encounter. After landing in Quito, Ecuador's capital, we set out north on a four hour van ride to Otavalo, a largely indigenous town of ninety thousand people with a world-famous open-air artisan market. Since I am not much for shopping, I followed Sandra Morse and Julián Larrea, our Ecuadorian guide, to the Shaman Market, where we purchased a variety of supplies for our upcoming spiritual cleansing. From Otavalo, we traveled high into the heart of Ecuador's sacred Andean volcanoes to the small village of Carabuela, where we visited a family of powerful healers or *curanderos*. Don Esteban and Rosa Tamayo and their son, Jorge, and grandson, José, offered us generations of their shamanic healing powers.

The Tamayos live in a valley between three volcanoes: the male Imbabura and his two female companions Huarmeraso and Mojanda. Amidst these powerful mountains, land and water, the Tamayos performed a sacred ceremony using water and fire—the revered elements of Earth. They offered us their ancient Andean healing techniques and invited us to deepen our connection with Pachamama. Don Estaban spoke of his ancestral prophecy of bringing together the eagle, representing North American mind culture, and the condor, representing South American heart culture. He passed on the story his ancestors told him: Every five hundred years, the eagle from the north and the condor from the south come together to soar in the same sky, announcing our transition into a more universal and sustainable way of living and relating.

Drawing upon their pre-Incan traditions, the Tamayo family was a formidable force of shamanic power, each one adding unique talents and energies to the healing ceremony. They demonstrated the art of using their mores and customs in working with the power, energy and wisdom of the elements. They accepted our *huacas*—our gifts from the Shaman Market of flowers, candles, eggs, tobacco and liquor, to be used in the cleansing ceremony for balance and healing. They led us into their world along an ancient path of initiation and healing. Their ageless techniques were intended to heal our emotional, psychological and physical afflictions. According to Don Estaban, the shaman walks a path of light, *el camino illuminoso*. He explained when we walk in the light of our hearts, we are doing the work of the shaman, and our light leads the way for others to follow.

The cleansing ceremony began with Don Estaban requesting that Pachamama reveal the specific illness or imbalance afflicting me. This involved rubbing a candle over my body, then having Don Estaban examine the flame of the candle for a diagnosis. The ceremony also included battering the pollution out of my afflicted karma with a barrage of cigarette smoke, whacks with bundles of medicinal herbs, and showers of raw cane liquor sprayed from their mouths. They ignited the liquor as they spit, creating a kind of spiritual flamethrower. I was told to keep my eyes closed, but of course I disobeyed orders. It, as well as I, was a sight to behold!

After participating in the cleansing ceremony, I knew something had taken place within me. I had been shown the world from a very different point of view. At the very least, I had been knocked out of my everyday practice and thought patterns for a few hours. This proved to be an excellent cure for what ailed me, and the Tamayo family knew exactly how to deliver the goods. As I left Carabuela, I knew for certain it was my job to redefine my position as a Catholic nun and American educator. I knew as never before that "I am the only one who can be responsible for me."

It was early evening when we departed Carabuela and set out for the small indigenous Quichua community of San Clemente, located ninety-five hundred feet above the city of Ibarra, in the highlands of Imbabura. In 2000, in an effort to confront the poverty in which this native community had been kept for years, fifteen families, headed by Manuel and Laura Guatemal, decided to carry out a daring ecotourism project designed to share their culture and country with others. The group decided to stand in solidarity and live in community as they practiced the age old custom of *minga*. A *minga* is a collaborative, volunteer project usually consisting of working in the fields, restoring roads or constructing communal buildings such as schools, clinics, dining halls, soccer fields, etc.

While staying with Manuel and Laura Guatamal in their magnificent, hand-built home, I participated in the customs and rituals of the San Clemente community. I experienced firsthand the true meaning of kinship, as I witnessed their deep respect for Pachamama (Mother Earth). I stood on sacred ground with loving people in a deeply cooperative spirit. I experienced "church" on a level I had never known. I was now prepared to enter the Amazon Jungle.

As we drove from San Clemente to the town of Shell to board a bush plane for the jungle, I had time to reflect on my two powerful experiences in the highlands of Ecuador. In Carabuela, I had come face-to-face and soul-to-soul with ancient rituals that were completely new to me. I saw that healing could be emotional and spiritual as well as physical. In San Clemente, I witnessed unconditional giving within community totally different from the model I had adhered to as a nun. While I was far removed from my daily practices, I was still within my comfort zone. Yet as I left the highlands, I sensed this was about to change. I knew I was about to descend to the depths of the Amazon Jungle. I had no idea what to expect, but I felt I had flown high with the eagle and the condor, and was now "going under" to experience whatever came next. I knew it would be intensely personal and forever life-changing. As I prepared to move from my head to my heart, I had no idea I would be called to surrender my soul.

Flying over the Amazon Rainforest expanded my sense of scale. It was as if every broccoli stalk had volunteered to stand end-to-end and side-by-side as sentinels guarding and preserving the planet. It put me at a key spot at the center of the universe. It took me to a specific point in time and space where the evolution of life seemed to stand still. There I was, suspended in ecstasy.

After an hour plane ride, we landed on a small dirt runway in the village of Kusutkau. Celestino Antík, the community representative and school teacher, let all thirty-eight kids out of school to come greet us. Celestino took us to some canoes, and after an hour boat ride on the Pastaza and Kapawari Rivers, we arrived at the Kapawi Ecolodge.

Kapawi Ecolodge is owned and operated by the Achuar. It consists of twenty palm-thatched bungalows on stilts above a shallow lagoon. The lodge accommodates one thousand visitors per year and was built in accordance with the Achuar concept of architecture—not a single nail was used. Kapawi has an abundance of observable indigenous wildlife living in harmony with the Achuar community. Profits from this project provide jobs and economic support for the Achuar in Kapawi and its surrounding communities, thereby allowing them to thrive in their homelands, protected from outside oil, forestry and farming industries.

After a day's rest, we traveled by canoe to the village of Wayusentsa to meet Shaman Rafael Taish and participate in an ayahuasca plant medicine ceremony. When I went to the rainforest to drink ayahuasca, I knew what it was but I didn't how it would affect me. I didn't know it would be a total biological, emotional and spiritual transformation. I was a different person after drinking ayahuasca.

Ayahuasca opens your heart. It is a vine and leaf the shaman cooks into a tea. The first time I drank ayahuasca, I felt the pain I had inflicted on every human being throughout my lifetime—quite an awakening for me. I had no idea I was that brutal, that hard to live with. And then the stars overhead morphed into the faces of every kid I had ever taught. Fifty years of history flashed before me. As I took it in, I knew I had been forgiven. I knew they had forgiven me; they accepted me for who I was. They had seen more than my bitterness. I had given them something more than anger and hostility. It was a peace I had never known before. It was the first time this old nun, after sixty-eight years of looking for God in all the wrong places, finally found peace. I finally found Spirit—Creator Spirit—at home in nature, in the heart of the jungle. For the first time in my life, I knew I was enough. I knew I was finally at home in my heart, in the heart of Pachamama.

In the Amazon Rainforest, as throughout my life, I prepared myself to climb the steep, slippery slope out of hell. Fortunately, Pachamama had a simpler plan to introduce me to her power and grace. In a single moment, the anger and depression of my past collided with the worry and anxiety of my future. There I was, suspended in the quiet of the present moment. I simply leaned into Pachamama and rested in her loving embrace. It was never about effort; it was always about effortlessness, surrender, letting go. As I accepted myself in the moment, I experienced peace, perhaps even ecstasy, for the very first time.

There in the jungle, Pachamama introduced me to a whole new level of consciousness. When I stopped judging and began loving, I found compassion for myself and all creation. As the Achuar shared their wisdom, culture and rituals, I found peace simply by following the native practice of receiving and offering forgiveness and peace to my ancestors as well as myself.

I knew I would have to return to reality and my relationships with my living kin, those people I love, appreciate, tolerate and sometimes resent. Now came the true test of personal conversion. Upon returning home I was amazed to find my friends and enemies had also changed. What trip did they take?

Once I changed my perceptions about me, I was able to change my perceptions about them. Once I forgave me, I was able to forgive them. Once I loved myself, I was able to extend love to them. I knew my next quest would be spiritual rather than intellectual. My next journey would be inward in service to my soul rather than outward in service to the world. I instinctively knew prayer and silence were portals for my transformational journey from darkness to light; from death to life.

When César Chávez Learning Community closed I was sixty-eight years old. Everything I had worked to achieve in life was brought down in a moment, leaving me feeling absolutely disgraced. Throughout my life, I had been able to manipulate intelligence, creativity and determination into the illusion of success and happiness. Stripped of my identity as an intelligent, creative person and successful educator, author and nun, Pachamama—the Spirit of Mother Earth—claimed my brokenness and blessed me with her peace and grace.

At the moment I drank ayahausca, I began my transformational journey from darkness to light; from self-hatred to self-forgiveness and, eventually, self-love. Pachamama "called me by name" (Isaiah: 43-1, NIV) and set me on a path that would lead to serenity and harmony with self and the universe. Finally, I was heading home.

Shouldn't an Old Nun Already Know How to Pray?

I went to therapists for years to complain that my life was unmanageable due to incidents that ruined my childhood and early life as a nun. I can't imagine how much time I spent wallowing in self-pity, seeking assistance only to prove no one could actually help me. I consistently rejected the belief that living in integrity—wholeness—was the goal of life. I perpetuated the myth that the weak and the wounded eventually win. I believed that brokenness was the best way to attract people to me. Fortunately, nobody tried to recover my fragmented pieces, and the more embattled I became, the less compassion and sympathy people offered. Nobody wanted to witness my pain, let alone reaffirm its reality by helping me carry my self-created burdens through life.

It took years to dispel the notion of the God of my childhood. I prayed to get things I wanted. I operated from the belief that, if I did good things, bad things wouldn't happen. God was my lucky rabbit's foot. Over many years, I morphed my prayers into consciousness, energy, light, drumming, talismans, power animals, talking in tongues, chanting, movement, dance and random acts of kindness. Yet no matter what I did, my prayers were still rooted in the idea of reciprocity; that if I contributed something I could expect to get something in return. It was not that these activities lacked godliness, but rather my participation in them originated in my mind, fed my ego and conveniently bypassed my soul.

Throughout my years as a nun, I slowly lost connection with my soul, and allowed events and circumstances to move me to a place of profound sadness. Lacking the skills to cope with dignity and grace, I slipped further and further away from my center. I lost what the Achuar call Arutum—my soul—the energy of life itself, the force that creates communion and hope, the vigor that enables one to move forward into an optimistic future. My connection with nature, life and God had dissipated. It was not until I searched for and eventually found Creator Spirit in the Ecuadorian rainforest that I arrived at acceptance, contentment and peace.

On the bank of the Kapawari River in Ecuador's Amazon Rainforest, I took off my shoes and stood on holy ground, without preparation, words or the need to bargain. A nearby palm tree offered a leaf and I lay upon it. In full and total humility, I finally uttered my first true prayer: "God, help me."

In that moment, the spirit in me pushed my tormented humanness to truth, and for the first time I realized hope was as powerful as despair. As I lay suspended in silence, benevolence replaced all the malice I ever put into the world. Grace diluted my anger and replaced my grief with peace. From the depths of my soul, Pachamama whispered without words, "Welcome home, Sister Jaguar, welcome home."

My Amazon Awakening

When I participated in the ayahuasca plant medicine ceremony with Rafael Taish, the Achuar shaman whom I came to know and love, Pachamama sent me the vision of the jaguar, whereby I experienced the recklessness of my anger. During my experience, I saw Pachamama's rivers run with blood and her plants and bushes turned to skulls. Yet Pachamama offered her tender embrace in my visual journey. Vibrating lines of vertical energy shimmered across my field of vision, candlelight shot outward in all directions like a re-enactment of the Big Bang, and colorful spider webs held planets and people in place.

Ayahuasca is more than a shamanic tool. It is the source of wisdom, the spring of knowledge for the entire society of tribes living in the Amazonian basin. To participate in the sacrament of ayahuasca is to heal and be healed. It is the vehicle by which Pachamama offered me direct experience with the Divine. In a single moment, she set me on a path to peace. For the first time in my life, I was excited for the possibilities of living in the here and now. I loved being suspended in this place of grace.

I am often asked, "Do you think you would have found God without going to the Amazon Jungle?" It's a good question. If it had been my destiny to find God in the Arizona desert, I would have done so. However, I believe it was her intent that I find her in the Amazon Jungle because that is where we met each other. To know God is to have a personal experience and relation-ship with Divinity. Of this I am certain: Pachamama chooses to meet every one of her children! "I have called you by name. You are mine." (Timothy 1: 1-14).

It took the skills of Sandra Morse and the grace of Pachamama to show me that *my story*—the ongoing narrative of my life's struggle—was fed by self-created fear, resentment, loneliness and anger. I slowly replaced my feel-ings of being *less than* with self-forgiveness and eventually self-love. Forgiv-ing myself, and then loving myself, gave me the power to change my story and commit to choices of improvement. This is my miracle. Miracles don't just happen. Everyday, I recommit to doing the work that will continue the miracle. This is spirituality.

I am reminded of the question I asked myself when my mom and I expressed regret, and requested forgiveness of each other: "Did it take all this for healing to happen?" Yes, it did. That's just how powerful my ego was. That's just how glorious redemption is.

PART TWO

PACHAMAMA'S PEOPLE

Up Close and Personal

The Achuar are an indigenous tribe living in the Amazon River basin in remote jungles of Ecuador and Peru. One of our planet's most ancient tribes, the Achuar are the original custodians of the Amazon, which consists of nearly two million acres of pristine tropical rainforest. Six thousand Achuar live in sixty-five small communities of fifty to five hundred people along both sides of the border that separates southeastern Ecuador from northern Peru. The name *Achuar* means *the people of the swamp palm.*

The Achuar are a millennia-old indigenous dream culture. Their lives are the manifestation of their dreams; they change their lives by changing their dreams. *Dreaming* is a term used to describe how the Achuar portray their origins, beliefs and spirituality. It is a complex network of knowledge, faith, and practices derived from their stories of creation. Dreaming influences all spiritual and physical aspects of Achuar life.

The Achuar consider all life part of a vast, complex network of relationships, which can be traced back to a period of time during which the universe was shaped by the actions of their half-animal, half-human ancestral spirit beings. They believe that, long ago, these mythological creatures began human society. For the Achuar, these spirits are as much alive today as they were in the beginning of time. They will never die. They are as much a part of the land and nature as themselves.

The Achuar live in a distant, inaccessible part of the Amazon Rainforest that has hardly changed in a thousand years. They had no contact with the outside world prior to the early 1970s, when they learned the modern world wanted the oil that "sleeps beneath their feet." Through their dreams, they intuitively knew the oil operations would destroy their environment and their very existence. The Achuar were emphatic that they did not want exploratory or extractive activity in their territory. They wanted to live in a sustainable way while preserving their values and traditions for future generations.

The Pachamama Alliance, Inc., a San Francisco based NGO, assists the Achuar in defending their cultural and territorial rights to live as their ancestors did, in an unspoiled part of the greatest rainforest on Earth. Somewhat ironically, the Achuar use ecotourism on a controlled, limited basis to preserve and protect their way of life. As they commune with nature and the modern world, they invite us, the people of the North, to understand, appreciate and share in their wisdom and rituals regarding environmental balance.

The Achuar have opposed oil companies from the United States, Canada and China, which conduct seismic testing and operate wells in the Cofán territory along the border of Ecuador and Columbia. The Achuar have said NO to oil drilling on their ancestral territory, and they are calling upon us, the global community, to support and assist them in this noble quest. In helping to protect the Achuar and their rainforest, we protect ourselves as well. The Amazon Rainforest is the lungs of Pachamama. Under the watchful care of the Achuar, the rainforest absorbs huge amounts of carbon dioxide and expels oxygen, thus allowing Pachamama and all of us to breathe with ease.

I remember the buildings and roads of the small town of Shell (named for its founder, the Shell Oil Company) quickly disappearing as the bushplane flew over the sprawling canopy of trees, deep into the heart of Ecuador's Amazon Jungle. As the plane landed on the remote dirt runway, our guide, Julián Larrea, commented that the closest town was a strenuous ten day hike from where we'd landed. After another hour by motorized canoe on the Pastaza and Kapawari Rivers, our group arrived at the Kapawi Ecolodge.

Upon arriving, I immediately began trying to learn what I could of the Achuar's native language. *Tsawarumek*—good morning, *maketai*—thank you, *winiajai*—excuse me, *nairka Judy*—my name is Judy, *wikia Americana*—I am American. It wasn't much, but I think they appreciated my effort. Over the years, Sandra Morse has developed close and meaningful relationships with many people in various Achuar villages. Word spread via shortwave radio that Sandra had come to visit.

On one visit, Achuar elders of the Wayusentsa village publicly thanked and honored Sandra as "one of them." They specifically asked that she help them organize projects whereby members from five Achuar villages might increase their protein intake in the form of chicken and eggs. They asked that she aid them in enhancing their children's education through the acquisition of specific school supplies, and in reforesting the trees along the edges of the villages, which had for decades served as firewood and shelter. Finally, the Achuar asked Sandra to assist them with simple technology needed to acquire rainwater for drinking.

Since that first visit in 2009, I have had many opportunities to accompany Sandra in visiting the Achuar in the villages of Kapawi, Wayusentsa, Kusutkau and Sua. The Achuar are a very gracious people and I am honored they offer me a level of friendship deeper than the warm interactions they extend to one-time visitors.

The jungle gives the Achuar everything they need to survive. The rivers and forests provide water for bathing, as well as fish, animals, wild fruits, insects and mushrooms to eat. Typically, the Achuar do not drink water, but rather *chicha*, an alcoholic beverage made of fermented manioc roots. The river and forest also provide all materials they require to build their large oval houses and make canoes, baskets, stools, ceramic bowls, bags, feather headbands, musical instruments and other items they use on a daily basis.

An Achuar house is inhabited by a single large family. The *jea* (house) is built exclusively by the men. A massive, intricately constructed palm-thatched roof covers the large, elliptical open-walled area, which has a natural dirt floor. Each house is built along an imaginary axis from west to east, or upstream to downstream. This orientation establishes the guidelines for dividing the house into social areas along gender lines: the male *tankamash* or west area and the female *ekent* or east area. Visitors are instructed to enter the house through the west end of the *tankamash*.

The *tankamash* is an eminently male area, where women are not allowed, except when serving *chicha* to the guests. Physical contact between men and women in the *tankamash* is prohibited. The man of the house sits on a *chimpui*, a wood seat carved in the shape of a tortoise, while receiving visitors. The *ekent* is inhabited primarily, but not exclusively, by females. No male visitor is ever asked into the *ekent*, but the man of the house has free access to this female space. The *ekent* is where the fireplace is located and all meals are made, including the preparation of *chicha*. The fireplace consists of three or four massive logs laid on the ground, almost touching at one end, while stretching outward. The fire burns where the logs are almost touching. As the logs burn, they are pushed closer and closer to the fire where hot coals glow continuously. Family members straddle the logs like park benches.

The *ekent* also contains the beds, each of which consist of a four-foot by eight-foot bamboo platform on stilts about three feet off the ground. Every woman in the house sleeps with her own children. The bed is the only place in the house where physical contact may take place, but rarely sexual relations, which are generally conducted in the privacy of the forest. Polygamy among the Achuar occurs, but is practiced less and less as the young men find it difficult to provide for more than one wife and numerous children. Within polygamous households the adults practice modesty and reserve.

Upon entering the *tankamash*, I often hear the Achuar man shout *"nijiamanch,"* requesting that his wife bring him a bowl of *chicha*. The man's wife instantly appears with a *pininkia*, a delicate earthenware bowl decorated with red and black geometric patterns. Slowly approaching her husband, she holds the *pininkia* with one hand and swirls the white liquid with the fingers of her other. She kneads and sifts the paste that has sunk to the bottom of the bowl, discarding thin fibers that float to the surface.

It would be unthinkable for a visitor to refuse a bowl of *chicha* when it is offered by the woman of the house. Such a gesture would insinuate distrust, implying that she may have poisoned the brew. It is important to accept the *chicha* with as much reserve as it is offered. The server does not make eye contact as she offers the refreshment. Under no circumstances should a male stranger to the household look at the Achuar woman when she hands him the drink. Such action could be mistaken as seductive behavior. Even the husband turns his head away as he holds his *pininkia* for his wife to refill.

This yeasty, alcoholic brew is central to the Achuar diet, often a substitute for food and water. From the cultivation of the manioc root, to the long hours harvesting clay from the river and decorating the ceramic bowls in which it is served, *chicha* plays a fundamental role in Achuar life and identity. The Achuar women exercise complete control over the making of *chicha*. The process is a crucial cultural skill, passed down from mother to daughter around the age of ten. The woman first peels, hacks and boils the manioc in a large pot, then chews it arduously, her saliva providing the fermenting agent. She continues to chew until the root turns to fine liquid, which she strains through her teeth and spits into a second pot. She then uses a paddle to mash the liquid into a smooth paste, and allows it to continue fermenting under a cover of plantain leaves. Just as each woman has her own personal *chicha* pot, each woman gives her brew a distinctive, personal touch. One woman's *chicha* might be smooth and sweet while another woman's *chicha* might be fibrous or sour. Achuar women are admired and sought after for the quality of their *chicha*.

When *chicha* is not fermenting in large clay pots on hard dirt floors, it is being cultivated, sung or whispered to, harvested, or doled out in homes and communal gatherings. Some men drink as many as six bowlfuls in a single sitting, or as much as three or four gallons a day, often skipping meals.

❧

Every Achuar family has a large garden, called a *chakra*, maintained solely by the women and girls of the household. They grow crops such as manioc, plantain, chonta palm, guava, papaya melons and avocado. Crops are often used to make medicines, body paint, adornments and household utensils. Among all plants grown, the Achuar believe manioc, guayusa and tobacco are most crucial to nurturing their bodies, minds, and souls. Manioc is the staple food of the Achuar, and is to them what bread might be to modern cultures.

Gardening is fundamentally a spiritual activity within the Achuar community. Crops are watched over by *Nunkui*, the spirit who created cultivated plants and controls the garden. The Achuar women develop relationships with *Nunkui,* and with the plants in the garden. They sing *anents* or magical prayers to the plants, referring to them as their children. These songs are extremely personal and are often sung in secret. Each *anent* has the same simple chirping melody but different lyrics. Women find solitude in their gardens and express their grief and suffering in private since public emotion is discouraged. Until recently, women gave birth alone in their gardens. The Jungle Mamas, an organization supported by the Pachamama Alliance, has empowered the Achuar to develop a midwife program for themselves.

I found the Achuar men to be present, confident and gracious. The women seemed distant, shy and industrious, with little facial expression and a seeming aversion to eye contact. The children, inquisitive and playful, initially keep their distance while peering at visitors from behind huge wooden posts that support the massive roofs on communal buildings. Their hesitation dissipates quickly, however, and the kids approach visitors, trying to get a glimpse of themselves on the screens of our digital cameras.

Other attributes of the Achuar people became apparent only after many days of interactions over the course of several visits. As they began to trust me on a deeper level, they allowed me to witness emotions such as worry, vulnerability, grief and anger, here displayed as a fierce determination to save their land and culture.

The Achuar do not have a political, hierarchical society like the power-down mentality that governs and entraps Western society. Perhaps, since family status has priority, community leaders do not rise to prominence. Upon closer inspection, it becomes clear certain men have subtle leadership roles within the community. Villages with shamans seemed to be larger, with more activity and influence than villages without shamans. The accessibility of villages along the river make them more easily and frequently visited than those located more inland. The entire village seems to come alive as visitors approach.

Throughout the day and into the night, the Achuar men focus on hunting and fishing. Some have rifles; all keep machetes and blowpipes. They kill animals in moderation, and show respect for every animal that gives its life that they might live. Prior to hunting or fishing, the men drink guayusa tea and share their dreams that foretell their success relative to an upcoming hunt. The men can often be seen transporting huge bunches of plantain by canoe. The long, straight trunk of the Kapok tree is used to make dugout canoes, a process that takes several months to complete, even with twelve men working together. When home, the men weave baskets or meticulously wrap the floss from the Kapok tree around darts for use in their blowpipes. They use the toxin of poison arrow frogs to coat their darts, of which even a small amount is lethal to humans.

The Achuar women tend to the children and gardens, in that order. The women and girls transport water from the river to the village on a daily basis. Even very young girls assist with the women's work. It seems to me that the young boys are constantly playing. They are responsible for very few chores around the house. I have never seen an Achuar infant unattended. When young fathers are in the home, it is common to see them holding their infants while the older children climb all over their dads affectionately. Infants and very small children are never on the ground, undoubtedly for health and safety reasons. The babies and children do not fuss. They demand very little attention, but on the other hand, they are continuously in the arms of or playing near someone who loves them. In the Achuar community, a crying child is a sick child. The Achuar women do not readily, if ever, offer their babies to visitors. In fact, Sandra Morse is the only visitor I have ever seen hold a variety of babies on a regular basis. The trust between Sandra and the Achuar is profound.

At day's end, the men play soccer or volleyball with nets hand-woven from plant fibers, while the children devise more cooperative games using a deflated, discarded ball. As always, the women serve *chicha* to the men and attend to the infants while visiting quietly with each other. Activity morphs into slumber just after twilight. A new day begins with the drinking of guayusa tea and the sharing of dreams before dawn.

Toward the conclusion of our two day visit, villagers and guests meet under the thatched roof of the common area for the traditional cultural exchange ceremony. I am always uncomfortable with this part of the inter-action because I have no authentic talent to share with anyone. In those moments, I think of my violin and how I might have put it to good use playing for the villagers.

The Achuar begin with storytelling, or more specifically, a conversa-tion between an "outsider" seeking entrée into the village, and an elder who decides if the request is justified. The two men, holding spears, sit face to face as they banter back and forth. I enjoy this strong, fast-paced dialogue, and the villagers, especially the children and teenagers, seem to love the continu-ous mocking and bragging. Next comes our poor rendition of *America's Got Talent!* Different members of our group take center circle. Those of us who don't make a habit of performing get up alongside those who can actually sing, dance or play a musical instrument with a modicum of ability. The entire group closes with our best stuff, which usually ends up being the Hokey Pokey. We "shake it all about," reveling in this coming together of vastly different cultures.

Finally the Achuar women take center circle, singing songs quite similar to the high-pitched anents of their gardens, as they hold hands and march in place. I cannot tell if the women are mimicking the clamorous chirping of birds at dawn or the nocturnal, strident chorus of frogs and crickets at night. It seems to me the birds, frogs and the women make sounds that are way too big for them. Whatever the sound, it is loud, shrill and braying, seemingly lacking an identifiable melody.

The talent show is always followed by a lavish dinner, Achuar style. The main course is manioc, which in celebration of our visit, is boiled and mixed with chicken, fish, or other game, if available. Next come fried plantains and hearts of palm served in rolled palm leaves. I have heard the Achuar also eat rice, corn and quinoa, but have never actually observed this.

After dinner, the Achuar women display homemade artifacts consisting of pottery, jewelry and wooden spears. A gift can be purchased from five to twenty dollars, the money from which is used to buy supplies, usually clothes and household items, from the Peruvian traders who travel the rivers on houseboats.

The Sua Salon Experience

On one particular visit, we noticed the older Achuar men and women sported the same jet black hair as the children and young adults. When Sandra inquired about this phenomenon, village elders laughed and explained that the milky juice of the *sua* fruit is used to darken the hair of the older members of the community. The sua fruit looks similar to a small green apple, with large dark seeds resembling those of a pumpkin. Sandra then arranged for our group to travel to the small Sua community for an indigenous hair-dying session. The Sua village consists of only ten *jeas* (houses) with large extended families. We were greeted by one woman and what seemed like all the children in the village. As communication along the river is often difficult, the woman we were told to meet had no idea we were coming. As she slipped into the forest to gather the needed fruit, we played soccer and hopscotch with the children. We watched as the young boys climbed nearby trees to cavort with monkeys, the closest thing they have to pets, as far as I could tell.

Upon our host's return, the Achuar woman showed us how to grate the sua fruit, producing a slightly milky juice. As our "beautician" squeezed the juice from the pulp onto our heads, liquid flowed down our faces and onto our clothes. Only after the seemingly innocuous sua juice had settled on our scalps did we realize what had really happened.

With one exception, everyone's hair turned black, while our ears, neck and hands turned a rich, royal blue. As for me however, my silvery white hair turned a flaming orange. Six months passed before my Tucson hairdresser was able to restore my locks to their original albino splendor. I vowed never again to jump into instantaneous rainforest beauty treatments with Sandra Morse.

Achuar Spirituality

Self-control is highly valued among the Achuar. Adults exercise discipline and willpower in the home by avoiding sex, gluttony and even sleep. They also carefully manage expressions and emotions, especially in front of visitors. Similarly, avoiding eye contact and covering the mouth when speaking are considered displays of self-control.

The religious beliefs of the Achuar are a composite of shamanism, witchcraft, superstition and a smattering of conservative Christianity. The Achuar believe in something akin to karma, a spiritual connection and sense of duty to nature, in particular the plants and animals they acquire and consume as food. They consider it a sacrament to ingest plants that allow them to connect with their dreams and practice "soul journeying." For example, the men rely on dreams and visions to predict their success regarding hunting and fishing.

The traditional Achuar belief system does not support the notion of an afterlife because the Achuar do not distinguish between varying planes of existence. There is no separation between the natural and supernatural; the conscious and unconscious; life and death. Everything is one and every moment is now. While Christians and others believe in an immortal soul, most Achuar believe that after death, the *wakan,* or disembodied essence of the dead person remains suspended in time somewhere nearby.

On one visit, Tutrik Froilan Antík, a young leader in the Kusutkau community, described the traditional ritual of burying his father, an elder in the community. Tutrik buried his father in a shallow grave inside the house, in remembrance of his father's continuing presence as head of the family. Tutrik pointed to the long, wooden, three-sided box resting above ground that was once his father's bed. There was no stone or marker. He explained that his father "sleeps" with his family, just as he always did.

Even though Tutrik's father completed his mission on Earth, he is expected to continue helping from the other side by giving ongoing direction to various family members. Initially, he may appear in dreams in his earthly body. As time passes and he joins his ancestors, he may choose to appear in dreams and visions as an animal, tree, rock, mountain or river. To be buried at home is the highest honor bestowed on any member of the Achuar community. People strive to be recognized as honorable elders because they hope they will be buried in the family compound.

Other family members are buried randomly in the nearby forest without any markers. The physical structure of an Achuar grave is such that it blends into the natural surroundings after a few months. As a people, the Achuar have a special connection with everything that is natural. They see themselves as part of nature—they see all the things on Earth as partly human. The Achuar believe that, after death, specific body parts become autonomous and reincarnate as animals to roam the nearby jungle. The lungs may become a butterfly; the heart may become a bird. These animals become materialized forms of a person's soul. The Achuar recognize these specific animals and never hunt or eat them, for doing so would be committing an act of spiritual cannibalism.

The Achuar believe every person exists eternally *in the dream* before the life of the individual begins, and continues to exist when the life of the individual ends. Both before and after life, they believe the spirit-child within each person exists *in the dreaming* and is initiated into life by being born through a mother. Remember, the Achuar see their earthly surroundings as the source and destination of all life. Everything comes from and returns to the forest so it can, in time, come again. For the Achuar, all of life is a single, breathing being, not a composite of autonomous entities.

On one particular trip, as our group ascended the river bank at Wayusentsa and began walking the air strip toward the village, I saw the entire community had already gathered. Ordinarily the people would gather at the common area upon our arrival, especially when they realized Sandra was among the visitors. Yet this particular day felt different, and I sensed they were having a community meeting to which we were not invited. Walking with a long wooden stick I had pulled from the jungle, I was, as usual, the last one in the group to arrive. Holley Allen, a pediatrician from Massachusetts, slowed down so I could catch up. We had a clear vantage point from which to see what happened next.

As our group approached the Achuar community, a small woman broke from the circle and headed towards the house of the local shaman, Rafael Taish. She was carrying a baby in a blanket. The child's arms were opened wide but it did not appear to be moving. The woman passed within a few feet of us but made no eye contact. I whispered to Dr. Holley, "That baby looks dead."

Having visited the Achuar on previous occasions, I did not find it unusual that Rafael Taish and Sekunnia Tentets, his wife, immediately sought out Sandra Morse. However, it was highly unusual for them to approach Sandra while crying. Rafael explained that their granddaughter had died just minutes before our arrival. This was their second granddaughter to die in eighteen months. Furthermore, Maria, mother of the two deceased children, was dying of uterine cancer. Sandra and Sekunnia held each other as friends and mothers, and sobbed together. Rafael extended his arms around both women. The three either could not or did not see the need to control their anguish in public.

Our group stayed at the far end of the communal area so Rafael, Sekunnia and Sandra could conduct their "sorry business" at the opposite end. "Sorry business" is the term used by the Achuar to express sadness and grief at the loss of loved ones. I quickly realized the thin woman Dr. Holley and I had seen leaving the group was a very thin Maria, holding her recently deceased baby girl. I had met them both on a previous visit, and had taken several photos of them with Sandra.

To tell the complete story, I need to explain the close relationship between

Sandra and Maria, a mother-daughter relationship-of-sorts that united these two women from distant worlds. Over the years, Maria and Sandra developed a close friendship. Maria, being the shaman's daughter, had access to experiences and opportunities that other women in the village did not. Sandra and Maria were able to converse in Spanish without the need for a translator, and with time they became a bridge between visitors and the people of Wayusentsa.

On one visit, Maria told Sandra that, if permitted by her father, she wanted to go to the United States and live with Sandra's family in order to learn English, go to college, and eventually return as a leader to her people. Maria certainly knew to ask the right person, as Sandra replied "Yes!" without a second thought. When Sandra and I returned to the village six months later, Maria's dreams had vanished. She had married an Achuar man, José Wasum, and they were expecting their first child. The Achuar have a matrilocal society. That is, the men leave their families and villages and move into the houses and villages of their wives. They fight and die for their fathers-in-law, though they share no blood connection. This is the opposite of a patrilocal society where fathers, sons and brothers stay together, even after marriage, in order to defend and extend the family legacy.

Sandra suggested to Rafael that perhaps our visit might be inappropriate. We could leave and return in a day or two. Rafael would not consider such a thing.

Sandra, Dr. Holley and I were invited to Rafael's house to witness the mourning of Maria's baby. Maria rested on a nearby elevated bamboo platform. One of her sisters sat on the ground holding her own active infant, as she prayed over a bowl of green *tsaánk* (tobacco) soaked in water. As each member of the community knelt beside her, she took a mouthful of the solution, held the person's eyes open and spit a fine mist into them. Each participant winced, stood and moved away with closed eyes, grimacing from the pain. Everyone present participated, even the children, but no one cried.

Maria's sister then followed the procedure for the infant resting in her lap. I was uncomfortable with this, as I could see the procedure was quite uncomfortable, if not outright painful. Maria's sister took the liquid in her mouth, covered the baby's eyes and sprayed the back of her own hand. I was very relieved at what I saw as a merciful gesture. There will be plenty of opportunities for the baby to experience the pain and suffering associated with living. Fortunately for the child, that day's suffering had been postponed.

This ritual reminds the Achuar that pain, suffering and tears are synonymous with grief, but that after they mourn, they return to life with little mention of the memory. The Achuar do not linger on their loss, perhaps because death visits them so frequently. Or perhaps it's that the Achuar see this transition not as a loss, but simply a natural part of life.

Throughout the ceremony, I watched Maria lying in bed just a few feet from the group. She was grieving intensely. Dr. Holley told me Maria's death was inevitable, but not immediate. She had no pain medication. Fortunately, I never go to the jungle without a variety of medicines. I gave Dr. Holley all the pain medication I had. She explained the dosages and protocol to Maria's mom.

Sandra sat with Maria for some time. They spoke softly to each other in Spanish, with a continuous exchange of tears and laughter. It was a very tender interaction, one that deserved all the intimacy possible within that communal setting. Rafael and Sekunnia were again overwhelmed with grief as they said goodbye to Sandra, who was equally devastated. I took my cross and chain from my neck and placed it in the hands of Maria's mother. I squeezed and kissed her hands as I said goodbye. She knew I understood.

Sandra, Dr. Holley and I joined the others at the communal hut, where we spent the night. Before we left the village, Sandra asked Maria if she wanted us to send back anything by bush plane when we landed in Shell. As I mentioned before, the Achuar are people of few words and even fewer facial expressions. If they want something, they simply ask for it without emphasizing need or desire. If they receive something, they acknowledge your generosity while showing very little pleasure or emotion. Maria told Sandra that she wanted eggs, milk, oatmeal, bananas, toilet paper and a few over-the-counter medicines. When we arrived in Shell, most of the group went to the market to complete this treasure hunt, while Sandra and Dr. Holley headed for *la farmacia*. We paid for the supplies, gassed the plane and hired the pilot to return immediately to the jungle. Maria had her supplies that evening.

Upon returning home, I thought about Maria on a daily basis. After a few months, Sandra received word that she and her two daughters were finally united in peace.

Go with God and your two babies, Maria.

I am certain Tutrik mourns the passage of his father, just as Rafael and Sekunnia yearn for their daughter and granddaughters. José also grieves the loss of his wife and daughters. I know this because I have witnessed their sorry business firsthand. However, I also believe Tutrik, Rafael, Sekunnia and José accept that their loved ones have returned to Arutum, the soul of Pachamama, and will be guides for them, and appear in visions as they seek Arutum in the future. The transformed energies of their loved ones will shift into new forms of life in the forest, as they surround their living kin in new ways.

Please, Pachamama, may it be so.

My 'Kodak Moment' Almost Lost its Magic

It took a few visits to the Achuar communities before I could recognize individual families, that is, parents, children, grandparents and relatives belonging to the same family. Julián Larrea, our Ecuadorian guide from Quito, often appointed me group photographer because he knew I was taking photos for my book. The other visitors were asked to take photos sparingly, always asking permission of the people. My strategy involved photographing every family as they sat together on benches in the common area. Upon returning home, I could match photos of individuals engaged in activities throughout the village with their specific family. This approach would later prove to be of great benefit, yet also a bit of a problem.

After spending many hours with the Achuar, I believe the world they perceive and the world I experience are two different places, two different dimensions almost. It is I who lose something in the translation from their world to mine. For the Achuar, objects are not separate from each other. The world is a single breathing entity. When I look at the rainforest, I see a series of trees. They however, see *treeness*—the spirit or energy of trees—in their totality. I view the world like a jigsaw puzzle, attempting to push pieces together whether they fit or not. I refuse to relinquish control. By contrast, the Achuar view the world in its entirety. Nothing is separate; everything fits together. They as a people are one aspect of a single, living, breathing entity.

They share the power that flows through them.

The Achuar do not relate to our two-dimensional world of books, photographs and screens. As I showed them photos of the rainforest on my camera, they stared at the screen as if the series of pixels made no sense. I finally stopped showing them the images.

I believe if an Achuar and I looked at the rainforest, what I see could in no way compare to the grandeur perceived by them. It isn't even fair to say the Achuar "look at the rainforest." They *breathe* the rainforest; they inhale and exhale the rainforest on a cellular level. They *are* the rainforest.

There were, however, images stored in my digital camera that the Achuar found funny and memorable. These were the photos I took of them. The only thing they could identify on the flat screen was themselves. Not so much *themselves*, but various members of their family and community.

Then something unusual happened. Rafael Taish, shaman of the Wayusentsa community, requested that I bring him photos of his deceased granddaughters upon my next visit to the village. I assured Rafael I would do this. Little did I realize the problem I would cause in honoring Rafael's request. I made duplicate photos of Maria and her two baby girls for José, Maria's husband. I also brought at least one hundred and fifty additional photos to be distributed to every family in the village.

When I gave José his photos, he immediately took all the others. When I told him the other photos were a gift for Rafael, José motioned he would take the photos to Rafael's house. Unfortunately, that delivery did not happen as swiftly or directly as it should have. Word quickly spread to Rafael that Sister Jaguar delivered his family and community photos to the wrong person. It was not the photos but my actions that created a commotion. Fortunately, Sandra Morse, Julián Larrea, our Ecuadorian guide, and Ruben Chakai, our Achuar guide, quickly calmed all offended individuals.

I knew there was trouble when I saw Julián and Sandra walking swiftly from Rafael's house in search of José. I then spotted them escorting José, photos in hand, to Rafael's house. Later that day, Rafael looked at me and said something in Achuar. I assumed he was thanking me for the time, effort and expense of fulfilling my end of the agreement. When I asked for a translation

I was told that Rafael had said, "You did not keep your word!"

I was devastated, and went immediately to Julián and Sandra for support, only to find out they sided with Rafael and the rest of the local community. I felt a complete fool, like I was the only one who could manage to be told—in three languages no less—that I lacked integrity. The next day, just before we departed from the village, Rafael made an announcement to the community as he distributed the photos to each family. Everyone was delighted. I was both relieved and thrilled. Every mother and father came to me to express gratitude for the precious gift of family photos. I took the exchange to mean all was forgiven, though that may have been a loose translation.

The gift of photos was a profound learning experience for me. While the Achuar were delighted with their new family treasures, the photos also represented some kind of power; a currency of sorts. I am grateful this potential disaster was skillfully avoided.

My Transformational Journey
from Darkness to Light

I am often asked, "Why do you go to the rainforest? What do you seek?" I always answer, "I am searching for God." I chose the Ecuadorian rainforest as the heart of my search for the same reason the jaguar stalks the jungle. It is our destiny. Each time I journey into the rainforest, I feel as if I am traveling back in time, to that moment when humans evolved to a point where they first turned to each other for security, camaraderie and love.

I go to the Amazon Rainforest to connect with the Achuar, who defiantly guard the entrance to their pristine, natural habitat and simple local communities. It is an honor to experience their culture and witness their role in protecting and preserving Pachamama.

For the Achuar, Pachamama is the holy vessel that holds Arutum, God, the energy of life itself. Pachamama is the living womb in which Spirit surrounds and supports the Achuar as they renew and rebalance the world. Each time I meet the Achuar, I rediscover my own beginnings—my inner source of energy and peace.

The terms "God" and "Spirit" hold considerably different meanings for the Achuar, as opposed to Western, Christian perspective. For Christians, these words are biblical in origin. For the Achuar, the term Arutum existed for thousands of years before they knew of the Bible. Arutum is synonymous with *God, Supreme Being* and *Spirit*. It refers to *the force of life* itself, the cogency that fosters communion and hope, the energy that enables humanity to move forward into a brighter future. My soul is my essence, my vitality, my life force, my Arutum. It is what keeps me alive.

The Achuar also refer to *susto*—soul sickness or loss—caused by life's disappointments and traumas, and the disappearance of the natural world. In its simplest terms, *susto* might be the lethargy one feels on a cold, cloudy day. On a deeper level, *susto* refers to the soul sacrifices made in order to survive significant traumas of life. A person might disconnect so the body and psyche do not have to experience the full impact of negative circumstances, and depending upon the level of stress experienced, parts of one's soul may become "lost." This means the energy or essence affected by the trauma is no longer available to the individual. This protective response is a normal reaction to the severe traumas of life. According to the Achuar, these "energies" or "soul parts" often return on their own over time.

In Achuar communities, the shamans perform the ancient ritual of *soul retrieval* in order to return lost soul parts, thereby restoring health and normal function to an individual. This powerful healing technique has been brought into our culture, as a result of renewed interest in shamanism in modern society.

I Roam the Rainforest to Discover my Place within Evolution...

The story of human evolution is chronicled against the background of cosmic evolution. Human history is imbedded in the history of our planet and the cosmos. The human community is interactive with and dependent upon the Earth community. We must create a worldview that demonstrates reverence for all of life. There cannot be peace among humans without peace with the planet. Only through embracing this new perspective regarding our place in the extraordinary unfolding of Earth's history can we emerge with a renewed awareness of our role in guiding Earth's evolutionary process.

To participate in Earth's continued evolution, we must articulate a new understanding of human-earth-cosmic relations. We must put an end to our history of alienation and the destruction of Earth, and instead support the premise of a balanced, sustainable future. Only then will we emerge as planetary citizens with the means to support and heal ourselves and our world.

To the Achuar, the rainforest embodies everything in the natural world. Their lives are interwoven with the very fabric of creation. Everything and everyone are of equal value. Everything exists for the common good. To the Achuar, independence and autonomy are nonexistent. If they did exist, they would be life-threatening. Everything in nature, living and nonliving, natural and supernatural is connected, working together to create a balanced and sustainable planet and universe.

Wherever we experience the grandeur of nature, Pachamama reveals herself to us. Her plants, animals and rocks reflect her completeness. Consider truth, justice, free will, freedom and liberty, all gifts Pachamama bequeaths to her children. When we give to each other, when we care for and protect each other without expectation of recompense, we are fulfilling Pachamama's plan for us. Nature tells us much about Pachamama and about ourselves. Our response to her is reflected in our treatment of her gift of creation. All of nature is sacred ground. Communion is the sacrosanct meeting of everyone and everything. To safeguard Pachamama is to protect and preserve life itself. In the process of healing Earth, we heal ourselves.

In times of crisis, I often retreat into nature in order to tap into Pachamama's wisdom and grace. I wonder at her extraordinary variety. No two things are exactly alike, nothing is repeated; everything is sacred. When I am in pain, I ask Pachamama to take me deep within her. There, as in the secret hiding places of my childhood, I rest in the loving arms of my mother.

1 Roam the Rainforest to Participate in the Ongoing Story of Creation...

The Bible begins with the words, "In the beginning God created the heavens and the earth" *(New International Version)*. Prior to that, the universe was formless, empty and dark. As Creator Spirit moved over the abyss and spoke creation into existence, she made people so we could communicate with her and with each other. She gave us the whole Earth to care for and cultivate.

Pachamama expects us to steward Earth. Our story can no longer be about us and our ability to manipulate our world. It must be about us recognizing our place in the world; seeing ourselves as nature. We are no longer part of Earth; we *are* Earth.

I Roam the Rainforest to Explore the Power of my Dreams...

Achuar life is filled with rituals, beginning with the cup of guayusa *(why-you-suh)* tea during the morning dream ceremony. Dreams, considered random in the North, are believed to be "created" among the Achuar, depending on circumstances and needs. For the Achuar, dreaming is an extension of conscious thought. Dreams drive behavior and vice versa. Living one's dreams is not the same as living one's fantasies, and the differentiation has enormous personal repercussions.

The Achuar participate in daily guayusa dream ceremonies in order to communicate with Pachamama soul-to-soul in an ancient language that requires no words. The Achuar believe everything in the rainforest, whether mineral, plant or animal, has a soul or life force. Everything on Earth is in continuous transformation because Pachamama has a soul. She is alive! The Achuar believe thoughts and feelings, whether expressed or unspoken, also have souls. All life and energy—past, present and future—contribute to the unfolding story of creation.

Before I could learn from my dreams, I had to learn how to remember them. Each night, before going to sleep, I sit on the side of the bed, take several deep breaths and begin to relax. I close my eyes, and manifest the intention to remember my dreams, reminding myself they are as much a part of me as my conscious self. I also commit to keeping a dream journal—a pad and pencil beside my bed, expecting to remember and write down my dreams as soon as I wake. I date each entry. Over time, I am able to see patterns and recurring themes.

My favorite dreams are those where I find myself flying, out of my body and free from the physical limitations I experience when awake. I can instantly travel to different locations in time and space. In this super-conscious state, I receive creative insights related to questions and problems that have come up in daily life. In some ways I am more comfortable living in the meditative or dream state, called the fourth dimension, than living in the physical (third) dimension. In the fourth dimension, I am free of the mental and physical pain I experience in "real" life. The Achuar believe living in their dream state is their reality; living in our reality is an illusion.

I Roam the Rainforest to Find my Shamanic Presence...

The Achuar regularly travel into the forest to visit the mighty Kapok tree. Legend has it that Arutum resides in the Kapok tree. With a diameter of ten feet, it rises up to two hundred feet above the ground—higher even than the rainforest canopy. Its seeds, leaves, bark and resin are used to treat fever, asthma, dysentery and kidney disease. Yet the Kapok tree is more than a source of food, medicine and building material. It is a place of healing, consolation and connection with other beings, and has long been sacred to the Achuar. The shaman visits the Kapok, and returns with the vision and power to transform human-earth-cosmic relations.

Shamans believe everything in the world is alive, and connected in a mutually supportive way. For the shaman, everything with form or substance has a soul: humans, animals, trees, wind, mountains, galaxies, buildings, cities, organizations, tools, inventions—everything. All of reality has a spiritual footprint. The shaman shifts into a mystical dimension to communicate with these spiritual entities and brings back an unlimited amount of potential and power to the physical world. In connecting with the spiritual aspects of reality, the shaman works with many souls of nature, including ancestors, angels, spirit guides, plants and power animals.

It is this direct connection with the spiritual dimension of our universe that makes the shamanic practice sacred work. It is a way of life—a way of receiving and giving. It is a life of humility, gratitude and love, with an abundance of joy.

I Roam the Rainforest to Communicate with Grandmother...

Ayahuasca (pronounced *eye-a-*was*ka*), or *yagé*, is the revered plant medicine of the Achuar, as well as many other tribes that call the Amazon Jungle their home. Ayahuasca is also called the *Vision Vine, Spirit Vine,* or *Vine of the Soul.* The indigenous people of South America refer to ayahuasca as a sacrament, a doorway to direct communication with the divine energy of Pachamama. Ayahausca, thought to have a feminine energy, is affectionately referred to as Grandmother. It is my understanding that the terms ayahuasca, Grandmother, and Arutum are used interchangeably for God.

Ayahuasca is a medicinal tea, usually prepared by boiling the rigid, brown stem of the ayahuasca vine with the green leaves of the chacruna bush. Chacruna leaves contain dimethyltryptamine (DMT). Neither plant causes any significant effects when ingested alone. They must be consumed together in order to have the desired heart-opening effect. Ironically, while these two plants grow a considerable distance from each other in the jungle, they were meant to meet.

Shamans converse with Grandmother, who holds the spirit energy of various life forms. Grandmother allows shamans to shift, to journey into alternative states of consciousness. The journey is enhanced by prayers, chants and repetitive sounds made from tree branches, rattles and drums. As shamans ingest ayahuasca, they see through "new eyes." They heal illnesses and restore balance on the soul level. Healing in this case refers to replacing a dream of illness with one of wellness. Rafael Taish, Shaman in the Wayusentsa village, put it very simply: "Grandmother is a plant teacher. She tells you what you need to know."

Ayahuasca is a spiritual medicine that frees the soul and heals the body. The Achuar believe the world has many layers, all of which are inhabited by people, animals and spirits. Ayahuasca allows the Achuar to visit these realms to obtain wisdom and power from the yagé people, that is, their ancestors, angels and spirit guides. Ayahuasca is more than a shamanic tool. It is the source of wisdom for all the tribes living in the Amazon River basin. To drink ayahuasca is to learn and heal, as you directly experience the Divine.

I Roam the Rainforest to Seek Forgiveness...

Sadly, early explorers and missionaries judged the beliefs, lifestyles and rituals of native people to be incompatible with faith. My religious predecessors missed the simple and obvious fact that native people have always had a profound respect for creation, and therefore, Creator. Only recently has the world recognized that indigenous tribes are responsible for the conservation of Earth's rich biodiversity. Throughout human history, native people have served as keepers of the dream, and conscientious caretakers of Pachamama. They are responsive to her call and devoted to her needs. They are sensitive enough to walk gently upon her. They are disciplined enough to accept her limitations. They love her enough to call her "Mother." In the process, they are tenacious enough to fight for her rights—the rights of nature—meant to assure the survival of all life forms, ourselves included.

Initially, I went to the rainforest to seek the forgiveness of these native people whom my ancestors, Dominican explorers and missionaries, unjustly abused. Despite that the Achuar hadn't requested an apology, I humbly asked for their forgiveness. In return, they requested that I listen to and assist them in their struggle to remain authentic. It is my privilege and duty to do so.

It was the Achuar in the Amazon Jungle who showed me how to forgive my three brothers and Dominican Sisters by eliminating the negative energy within me, not them. Once I took responsibility for my anger, I had the power to change it. I knew I could change it because I created it. None of my negativity is anyone else's fault. To eliminate my anger and pain, I needed only to change myself. I found peace with my brothers and my Adrian Dominicans Sisters in a remote village in the Amazon Jungle simply by asking for and receiving forgiveness. When I forgave myself, I was able to forgive them. When I finally loved myself, I was able to extend love to others.

1 Roam the Rainforest to Take a Stand for Eco-justice...

Western society and industrial nations have inflicted significant—perhaps irreparable—damage to our planet, compromising its identity as a viable dwelling place for life through global warming and the pollution of air, land and water. We are responsible for holes in the ozone layer, the clear-cutting of forests, the endangerment and extinction of plants and animals, overpopulation and nuclear destruction.

We must expand social justice to include eco-justice. We do this by extending our attention to include not just humanity, but the whole community of life. Since nature is the *new poor*, our commitment to establishing justice for the impoverished must include all life systems and species under threat. We must support the belief that the value of standing rainforests is priceless, whereas the costs associated with their destruction are devastating. We must support social and economic development projects in South America. We must promote awareness of ancient cultures and indigenous spirituality in North America.

When I stand on the bank of the Pastaza River, I stand on the edge of *blessed unrest*—that state of undeniable connection and service to life. How did I get here, to this place, this moment in time, this edge on which I stand? Am I willing to address humanity's most pressing issues? Can I discover new ways of relating with others and with Earth? When I stand in solidarity with the Achuar in the Amazon Rainforest, I am in a position to bring about an environmentally sustainable, spiritually fulfilling and socially just human presence on this planet. If I am not standing on this edge, I am taking up too much space.

The questions of how and whether I will help heal Pachamama's wounds are not scientific or technological, they are personal and spiritual. Why do I do what I do? Do I use my time and skills wisely? Is my life all I had hoped and expected it would be? Am I fulfilling my destiny? Have I made positive contributions to the cultural, political, economic and social fabric of my community, my country and my world? Have I contributed to the happiness and fulfillment of Pachamama? Have I made her more peaceful, healthy and balanced?

Pachamama has given me the opportunity to participate as co-author of her creation story. In return for this honor, she asks that I give all other beings a chance to participate as well.

I Roam the Rainforest to Find Peace...

The Achuar believe home is a love song carried through the day by the sun and the night by the moon, forever dancing in harmony and balance. The journey through life is really the search for home. Home is not a connection to a particular physical place. It is where I belong emotionally. It is wherever I am rooted on Earth. It is the ground upon which I walk. It is the place of connection for my heart and soul.

Home changes as I change. Home is the place where I am at peace, where I am safe and open to whatever happens. Home is a feeling of warmth. It is a moment of truth. It is all that feels familiar and comfortable, yet inspires me to always and forever be more. Home is where my story begins and ends.

As I continue my journey, I make sure my footsteps fall gently upon Pachamama. As I kneel and lay upon her, I feel our hearts beat as one. I remember the sound of her wind that swirls above the mighty Kapok tree. I remember how she feels, how she smells, how she speaks, how she nourishes her children. I see her beauty, feel her power and know her peace. I listen to her ancient songs that need no words. I rest gently in her embrace, for I am home.

Final Comment

Iinstinctively knew the path to peace was an inner journey. As a nun, I
engaged in a variety of religious practices for seventy years with minimal
psychological or spiritual return. Then, in a single, simple, life-changing shamanic ritual in Ecuador's Amazon Rainforest, the heart-opening plant medicine I lovingly refer to as Grandmother suspended the clutter of my judging
mind.

Every prior experience in life, negative and positive, contributed to that
moment in time. Among the Achuar, I was able to dismiss my childhood, religious and cultural conditioning as well as all preconceived notions of myself
and the world. I simply surrendered as Pachamama drew me into the present
moment. There I rested in her loving embrace—heartbeat to heartbeat, in the
heart of the jungle. As I forgave and accepted myself in that moment, I experienced self-love, Pachamama's peace on a primal, pristine level.

Most gurus and spiritual masters would say that peace is the byproduct
of years of intense effort and discipline related to meditation. Fortunately, I
found an easier path to *contemplate alies traderae*—the fruits of contempla-
tion. Pachamama afforded me a sacred place where I was able to merge with
her. In the Ecuadorian rainforest, in the heart of Pachamama, I tapped into
her soul and mine, as self-forgiveness and love flowed to me, through me and
beyond me.

All my life I engaged in pseudo-personal reformation, always skirting around the edges of perspectives I held that were truly toxic. It was not until Pachamama touched my soul with hers that I knew peace and experienced ecstasy for the very first time. I was able to find peace through self-forgiveness and love at the center of my being. When I stopped judging and began loving, I found compassion for myself and all creation. In prayer, my heart accepted myself and others without manipulation or reservation.

Today, whether praying in Amazon's rainforest or Arizona's desert, I am able to submerge myself in nature without getting lost in specific thoughts or judgments about it or myself. Wherever I am in nature, Pachamama hushes and heals me. As we commune, she offers me her Arutum, her healing energy. We are one. I am home.

While you could say I found peace in the heart of the Amazon Rainforest, it would be more accurate to say I found peace in the present moment. After prowling the planet for seventy years, this old, tired "jaguar" finally found peace in a prayerful journey to the center of her being.

I have asked Sandra to mix my ashes with the soil beneath a mighty Kapok tree in the Amazon Rainforest. When I return, I hope I don't need to wander seventy years before realizing and fulfilling my purpose. I expect to begin again at *home*, that place that took me a lifetime to discover, that place of forgiveness and peace at the center of my soul.

Alphonse "Babe" Bisignano and Catherine Dwyer married January 23, 1934.

Babe Bisignano celebrates his 80th Birthday with four of the five Biz Kids, 1983.
Left to Right: Joe, Jim, Babe, Sister Judy and John.

Top: Sister Mary Alphonse, BVM as a novice, 1959. Mary Kay died November 9, 1964 at age 23.

Middle: Last photo of SIster Judy with her mom, 1979.

Bottom: Sister Judy with her mom in the early 1970s.

Judy as postulant – the first step to becoming an Adrian Dominican Sister – August, 1960. Left to Right: Jim, Sister Judy, John and Joe.

Becoming a novice – prostration ritual, 1960.

Professed nun, 1965.

With Kino Kids, 1972.

Sister Judy with parents greeting Pope Paul VI at summer residence in Castel Gandolfo, 1970.

Kino Learning Center has been a radical model of alternative education in Tucson, Arizona since 1972.

Kino Learning Center is a one-room schoolhouse where children ages 5-18 engage in project-based learning.

Located on ten acres of magnificent desert land, Kino Learning Center includes a nature trail, greenhouses, gardens and an animal center.

Photo Credits:
Nancy Bachelier

Top Left: Students at César Chávez Learning Community prepare an altar for Día de los Muertos, Day of the Dead.

Top Right: ¡Sí se puede! Yes we can!

Bottom Left: Students regularly marched for their immigration rights.

Bottom Right: The arts played an important role in the lives of the students. Here the mariachi group performs locally.

Top Left: Don Estaban and Rosita Tamayo prepare for our cleansing and healing ceremony. Their son, Jorge, and grandson, José, are also shamans.

Top Right: Manuel Guatamal of the San Clemente community introduces Julián Larrea, our Ecuadorian guide, to his Kichwa kin.

Bottom Left: The San Clemente community shares their Kichwa music of the Andean highlands.

Bottom Right: Manuel Guatamal demonstrates the two methods he uses to call the community together.

Photo Credits: Sister Jaguar

We enter the Amazon Jungle with an hour plane ride over the Achuar territory, the lungs of Pachamama.

Shaman Rafael Taish of the Wayusentsa community offers a blessing as we arrive at the village.

Legend has it that Pachamama's Arutum (spirit) lives in the mighty Kapok tree.

Photo Credits:
Top: Patricia Dolan
Middle: Sophia Lyn Sims
Bottom: Sophia Lyn Sims

Top Left: Sister Jaguar with orange hair and blue skin after the Sua hair dying experience.

Top Right: Sandra Morse leads immersion experiences in the Amazon Jungle for the Pachamama Alliance, Inc.

Bottom Left: While the group hikes in the rainforest, Sister Jaguar waits in the canoe.

Bottom Right: Julián Larrea lends a helping hand to a tired, old jaguar!

My proof reader
in the Amazon
Jungle!

I never intended to write a book.
I sat at river's edge and
waited for my friends who were
hiking the rainforest. Soon my the
thoughts in my head reached my
heart and poured on to note paper.
The result was Prayers from the
Rainforest. Sister Jag's Journey did
not materialize until much later.
Here are a few of these prayers.

Sister J.

PART THREE

PRAYERS FROM THE RAINFOREST

Prayers from the Rainforest

1. Finding Arutum (God) in all Creation

Opening Prayer:

Pachamama, I seek to renew my relationship with you and your timeless values that have been kept alive by the Achuar and indigenous cultures since the beginning of humankind. Give me their vision of you that originates in the depths of their souls and extends to the celestial regions of the cosmos.

Let me learn from my ancient ancestors how to develop and expand my shamanic (healing) consciousness and join with them as co-creators of peace and harmony within nature and among your people. Let our ancient and modern cultures come together in search of common resolutions to our planetary problems.

Introduction:

For the Achuar, God is a feminine energy. Her name is Pachamama (Mother Earth) and she is the living womb that holds Arutum—the Creative Spirit that surrounds and supports them. The Achuar recognize fully their role as co-creators of the universe. Arutum is the energy through which they renew and rebalance the world.

Achuar spirituality is expressed in everyday life as solidarity, that is, communion with the whole of creation. Their vision of Pachamama is based on mutuality—life in relation to everyone and everything. In their view of the cosmos, the Achuar find God in all creation, in all that generates life and enables community. In their world, nature and Pachamama are a single entity through which they seek balance and harmony. They use natural materials in ritual to launch themselves to levels of altered consciousness, always within the splendor and simplicity of nature.

Reflection: I am part of Arutum, the sacred energy of life.

The concept of co-creation suggests that I and all life forms are involved in what happens. I participate in the ongoing creation process with and through

Pachamama. When I tell the universe what I want, when I envision the life I want to live, I create or initiate this reality for myself. When I request the assistance of Pachamama, I expect her support and she requires my cooperation. Grace occurs and miracles happen when divinity and humanity join together to further good in the world.

The Achuar are never alone. They are continuously in the presence of Pachamama, who causes the dawn to break and the sun to set. Waking in the morning is proof of the existence of Pachamama, who allows them to experience a new day, to see the river flowing, the plants growing and the children playing in the forest. To experience nature in its magnificence and splendor is to know and be in the presence of Pachamama.

- As I appreciate and respect indigenous cultures and the richness of their mythic, symbolic and religious life, I am part of Arutum, the sacred energy of life.

- As I realize what happens in one place ultimately affects everyone and everything, everywhere, I am part of Arutum, the sacred energy of life.

- As I am inspired by the simplicity and strength of indigenous communities that resist outside forces which threaten their borders, language and culture, that is, their very existence, I am part of Arutum, the sacred energy of life.

- As I realize I am in the human race and the human race, in all its diversity, is in me, I am part of Arutum, the sacred energy of life.

- As I deepen my awareness that every person on the planet is individually and uniquely connected to all other people, I am part of Arutum, the sacred energy of life.

- As I align myself with the forces of renewal, balance and regeneration that exist in the natural world, I am part of Arutum, the sacred energy of life.

- As I seek a harmonic relationship with Pachamama, who encompasses the sacred presence of Earth, sky, universe and time, I am part of Arutum, the sacred energy of life.

- As I live in communion with the whole of creation, I am part of Arutum, the sacred energy of life.

I seek wisdom to these questions:

- What has been the dominant image or name for God in my life? Jesus? Lord? Adonai? Spirit? Creator? Source? Can I incorporate new names and images such as Pachamama and Arutum?

- Can I find a new image of God for a centering prayer? *"Pachamama, let us nurture and protect each other."* Or, *"Arutum, let your energy transform me and your world."*

- What do I need to enter the heart of nature? How do I allow the heart of nature to enter me? Is there a difference between the two?

- What conversations unfold between my soul and Arutum, the soul of Pachamama?

- As I continue my sacred journey, Pachamama reveals that there is no going back to life as I once lived it. What changes are taking place in me as I move toward greater clarity of purpose and being?

Closing Prayer:

Pachamama, I see the world through your eyes. I have an understanding of the interconnectedness of all of nature. I have the authenticity and integrity to exist only within your spirit of interdependence. I have your sense of justice to foster reciprocity among your people. I offer deep reverence for them and you. You are my loving Mother. I am grateful for your nourishment and protection. I commit to sustaining you as I rest in your loving embrace.

Everything that comes into existence, living and non-living, is connected to everything else. Nothing exists solely on its own.

~ Shi Wuling

If you wish to make an apple pie from scratch, you must first invent the universe.

~ Carl Sagan

2. My Place in the Natural World

Opening Prayer:

Pachamama, I hear your voice in the wind as you call my name. Your breath gives life to the world, of which I am an active participant. Your rains shower me with fresh, clean water. Your thunder calls me to strength. Your lightening awakens my thoughts and brings clarity to my vision.

You have given me the wisdom of my ancient ancestors. You have taught me the lessons hidden in every rock, leaf and living thing.

Pachamama, I recognize my niche within your web of life. I am aware of your presence in me and in the world. When my life sets as the fading sun, my spirit will come to you swiftly with grace and love.

Introduction:

Nature provides a self-portrait of Pachamama. She is forever present, revealing her attributes: loving, nourishing, protecting and strikingly beautiful. Wherever I see the grandeur of nature, it is Pachamama revealing herself to me. Her plants, animals and rock formations reflect her completeness. Consider truth, justice, free will, freedom and liberty. All are gifts Pachamama bequeaths to her children.

Nature tells me much about Pachamama. My response to her is reflected in my treatment of her natural gifts. When I give to others, when I care for and protect others without wanting or expecting anything in return, I am fulfilling Pachamama's plan for me. It is my role to take the time and make the effort to go deep into nature, where I can experience Pachamama at her finest. Then, she will take me deep within her, to be consumed by her.

Reflection:

TO NATURE: As you sing Pachamama's love songs, your beauty reflects the magnificence of all creation. Your stillness brings me peace.

TO TREES: As your branches bless and protect me, I stand by you, anchored through the turbulence of life.

TO MOUNTAINS: I stand for justice and truth in all my interactions, as you stand unshaken yet forever changing throughout time.

TO SUNSHINE: The light and warmth of your glory shines in my heart. My soul rises with you in the morning and rests with you at night.

TO SKY: You rise up and encompass me as I experience your mystical presence.

TO CLOUDS: You reflect the light of the sun, as my soul reflects awareness of all Earth's inhabitants. As you disperse the sunlight, kindness radiates from me to all creation. As you engulf the light of the sun, you protect and comfort me in my darkest hours, for my darkness seeks your light.

TO AIR: I hear your voice, as the wind speaks divine messages to those who listen. I feel your loving caress as you lift me and carry me to divine places.

TO WIND: Fan the flames of my passion and compassion. Fill me as air fills the flute with song.

TO MOON: My life reflects the light as you reflect the sun. I grow in wholeness and holiness as your waxing progresses towards fullness. Your light is the torch that guides my path through the darkness.

TO RAIN: Shower your mercy, compassion and abundance on all living things. Everything that exists is alive on some level.

TO RIVERS: Your wisdom and joy flow into and through me as you rush to the sea.

TO STORMS: Anchor and ground me as you interrupt the calmness of my life.

TO FIRE: I live in your warmth. Purify my heart. Turn my ego to ashes. Kindle within me a passion for service to others.

TO ANIMALS: I communicate with you without words as I stand ready to listen to you and protect you.

TO HUMANS: I see Pachamama in every person, for she made us to look just like herself.

TO CONSTELLATIONS: My story reflects your myths and legends as I connect your stars to one another.

TO SPACE: I rise above worry and fear in your limitless presence. I greet you as formless and beyond restriction.

TO UNIVERSE: You are splendid, out of reach, beyond comprehension, simply there to let me marvel at your grandeur.

I seek wisdom to these questions:

- How does nature provide me with a self-portrait of Pachamama?
- How does my growing awareness and appreciation of nature contribute to the creation story?
- When nature and I go deep within each other, are we consumed by Pachamama? Do we become a single entity of life? How and when does this happen?

Closing Prayer:

Pachamama, bless all creation with your wondrous love. I commit to bringing balance to your world and healing to all its inhabitants, especially the poor and the suffering. I have the sensitivity to respect and care for you. I have the courage to use my technological inventiveness to undo the damage I have done. I recommit to being a faithful steward of your planet. I take responsibility to protect and sustain your handiwork.

When we return to nature and adhere to it, we are worthy.
~ Chou Tun-i

When the last tree and icecap are gone, and the last river has dried up, only then will humans realize that they cannot eat gold and silver.
~ Parshuram Tamang

3. Oneness of Nature and Humanity

Opening Prayer:

Pachamama, I am sorry for wounding you by polluting your water with chemicals, filling your air with soot and fumes and contaminating your soil with heavy metals and plastic waste. I have no right to view your rainforests as a cash crop to be harvested at the expense of its indigenous caretakers, rather than an irreplaceable ecosystem to be protected for all humanity. I am wrong to assume your resources and services are free and limitless. I regret that my choices for short-term gains have resulted in long-term costs and degradation of your planet.

Introduction:

Being human, I have a consciousness different from all other forms of life. I appreciate the beauty of nature, as well as mourn its loss. I find hope in the rising of the sun, moon and stars, and find peace in their daily passage. I recognize and appreciate flowers in bloom, water as it meanders through the Amazon, the strength of the jaguar and anaconda, the fragility of butterflies, trees blowing in the very wind they help to create. My relationship with nature inspires in me a sense of wonder and beauty that births an awareness of Pachamama.

Unfortunately, industrialization, urbanization and habitat loss have led me to a state of detachment from the natural world. I have reached the point in the evolution of the planet where my needs and wants are outstripping Pachamama's ability to provide. Pachamama is not in the habit of fixing my careless and arrogant mistakes. That is my job. The solution requires a conscious act on my part, for me to say "yes" to more constructive alternatives. I must commit as never before to healing Pachamama.

Reflection:

Reflecting on nature is not just an intellectual exercise. It involves feeling as well as thinking. Imagine what the Achuar might be thinking and feeling in the rainforest. For the Achuar, all things are interconnected, and therefore dependent on each other. When they look at a tree, they don't just think, "There is a tree." They have a personal relationship with each and every tree. They see trees as kin. Encountering a tree is like coming into contact with a close friend or relative.

The Achuar embrace the concept of the tree. They see the tree as a descendent from a seed on its way to produce more seeds. They see the tree as a product of conditions related to rain, sunlight, soil nutrients, etc. They see the tree as breathing the same air and drinking the same water as themselves. Fruit picked from the tree today will become part of themselves tomorrow. For the Achuar, the trees, the fruit and themselves are all part of a single whole. It is one entity; one existence.

Indigenous people have been living in harmony with their environment for millennia. They are informed by knowledge and guided by Arutum imbedded in nature and themselves. They view nature not as a collection of separate elements, but as an interconnected web, with each of us an integral component in the miraculous and fragile network of life.

There are times when I perceive the elements of nature as an interconnected whole, myself included. The Achuar, however, are continuously connected with Pachamama and each other. They are one with all of life.

- I call upon wisdom to see that the ecological crisis to which I have contributed is both a physical and spiritual one.
- I call upon prudence to adjust my values and practices in time to stop the planet's destruction.
- I call upon respect, for when I demonstrate self-respect, I honor the world.
- I call upon humility as I claim my position within the interconnectedness of all matter: living in the now of past, present and future.

- I call upon gratitude, for at the beginning of time, at the moment first light emanated from the Big Bang, I was birthed into existence as part of the whole of creation.
- I call upon serenity for allowing me to see myself as part of the interconnectedness of all of life.
- I call upon faith and the expectation it provides to fulfill my dreams for Pachamama and her people.
- I call upon hope, for when I heal Pachamama I heal myself.

Closing Prayer:

Pachamama, thank you for the ability to combine ancient and modern worldviews into a single vision; an alloy that blends modern science and intellect with the deep and ancient wisdom of traditional cultures.

I seek wisdom to these questions:

- How can I deepen my relationship with the miraculous and fragile network of life?
- How and when do I perceive nature as an interconnected whole, myself included?
- What are my hopes for the natural world? What is my role in making these hopes a reality?
- What can I learn about the relationship between indigenous people and Pachamama? Does this deeper awareness bring me closer to both Pachamama and her native people?
- How may I combine the deep wisdom and respect of the ancient world with the technology of the modern world into a single vision?

If the dreams that have guided us to a certain point become dysfunctional, then we must go back and dream again.

~ Thomas Berry

The Universe will reward us for taking risks on her behalf.

~ Shakti Gawain

4. Embracing Nature in Radical New Ways

Opening Prayer:

Pachamama, I commit to the three chapters of your story of creation. The physical Earth, the living world and the human community read as one interrelated love story. I have the wisdom and courage to call the members of my community into a more authentic mode of living and being. I will never lose a sense of the sacredness of your natural world. It has been my identity and destiny since the beginning of time. My ancient ancestors stood upright in order that I could bow to the magnificence, completeness and interrelatedness of you and your natural world. I promise never to bring our planet to its knees; to a place of environmental disaster and social disorder.

Introduction:

Before I can improve my behavior on an environmental level, I must recognize the tragedy I have caused Pachamama. I must acknowledge my passive acceptance and abusive behavior toward her. My appetite has increased the volume and speed with which her natural resources have been transported through the industrialized world and into junk piles and landfills.

I have witnessed the pulverizing of her mountains, the draining of her rivers and the flooding of her valleys. I have seen toxic chemicals poured onto her fields and grasslands until her soil blows away in the wind. I have watched her forests turn to consumable paper product wastelands. I have contributed to polluting her air with acids, her rivers with sewage and her oceans with oil.

Pachamama is at the tipping point. She is at the edge of *blessed unrest* between destruction and salvation. If we lose her divine presence, we lose ourselves as well.

Reflection: I have the courage to do Pachamama's bidding.

There is nothing wrong with the story of creation. Humans just refuse to see their rightful place within it. Today's creation story calls for a change in our worldview, wherein humans demonstrate reverence for all life. The new creation story fosters reciprocity among humans and reverence for the entire Earth community. It calls for an end to alienation among Earth's inhabitants. It requires a new context for connection and purpose. It offers a new orientation and perspective that suggests a moral basis for action. It calls for an emergence of a sense of planetary citizenship. It promotes the beginning of a sustainable future. It provides the human energy needed for positive social, political and economic change.

The creation story provides the narrative for human history in relation to Earth's history. Evolution and history merge to establish respect and mutuality among humans, and between humans and Earth. There cannot be peace among humans without peace with the planet.

The human race is between creation stories. That is, we have not yet fully articulated a new creation story for modernity. While a complete story has not yet been manifested, we know it must be rooted in sound human-earth-cosmic values. Our story cannot be about us and our ability to manipulate our world. It must be about us recognizing our place in the world; seeing ourselves as nature. We are no longer part of Earth; we *are* Earth.

- As I move from *social justice*—the rights of people, to *eco-justice*— the rights of people interwoven with the rights of nature, I have the courage to do Pachamama's bidding.

- As I see social justice and eco-justice issues as intertwined elements of how humans are called to relate to each other and the world, I have the courage to do Pachamama's bidding.

- As I realize it is not possible to care for people without also caring for the environment, I have the courage to do Pachamama's bidding.

- As I recognize that environmental quality is synonymous with quality of life for humans and all other life forms, I have the courage to do Pachamama's bidding.

- As I realize the Biblical call to "love my neighbor" is identical to the call to love nature and planet Earth, I have the courage to do Pachamama's bidding.

- As I understand more deeply how divine things manifest themselves in the physical world, I have the courage to do Pachamama's bidding.

- As I discover the human heart is not changed by information, but by empowering values and engaging visions, I have the courage to do Pachamama's bidding.

- As I develop a deep interplanetary consciousness and conscience, I have the courage to do Pachamama's bidding.

- As I embrace my embeddedness in nature in radical, fresh and enlivening ways, I have the courage to do Pachamama's bidding.

- As I acknowledge that humans, Earth and all life are bound by a single destiny and love story, I have the courage to do Pachamama's bidding.

Closing Prayer:

Pachamama, you have given me godly insight into my new identity and my timeless destiny as co-creator of your kingdom. I have the wisdom and courage to co-author your creation story. I have the tact and tenacity to call others to a more authentic mode of living and being. I have the humility to acknowledge and appreciate the magnificence, completeness and interrelatedness of your natural world.

Allow me new visions where I see everything and everyone within Arutum—the soul of Pachamama. Bring comfort and healing to all your creatures. Strengthen, energize and transform your world. Permeate your planet with love. It is time, Pachamama, it is time.

I seek wisdom to these questions:

- How, when and through whom does Pachamama reveal herself to me?

- How have I contributed to the tragic elements of the creation story?

- How can I help rewrite the creation story in ways that sustain and protect Pachamama?

- How do I embrace nature in radical, fresh and enlivening ways?

- How do I acknowledge that humans, Earth and all life are bound together by a single destiny and love story?

Let us bear the universe in our being just as the universe bears us in her being. Let us emerge not only as earthlings, but as worldlings.

~ Thomas Berry

We are not separate from the whole. We are one with the sun, the earth, the air. We don't have a life. We ARE life.

~ Eckhart Tolle

5. Rising into My Destiny

Opening Prayer:

When soft rays of light ascend over the trees, it is always as if for the first time. Clarity of purpose rises with the advent of a new day. Dawn beckons with the invitation to begin anew, to see things in fresh ways. "Yesterday is past," it whispers. "You have only today and all its possibilities." I join the Achuar by beginning each day anchored in stillness, taking nothing for granted; open to whatever the coming day's gifts may be. It is the beginning of a new day and a new dream.

The morning silence is filled with your breath, Pachamama. It draws from me a quiet prayer that leans on the presence of hope and requests that I seek you throughout the day. It all starts with the morning, the fertile soil that helps me realize my destiny to leave this world more whole and holy by day's end.

Introduction:

Dreams are the language of God spoken through the soul of Pachamama. Dreams allow me to recognize the immensity of life's possibilities. They allow me to articulate a personal legacy within local and global communities. Dreams allow me to identify and bring my unconscious thoughts into this present moment of ordinary reality.

Pachamama has chosen a life path, a destiny, for me. She desires that I achieve my destiny—my destination—before leaving this Earth. I become aware of my destiny by having the courage to confront my dreams. When I share my dreams, desires and destiny with Pachamama, she conspires to help me achieve them. When my intentions are pure by serving Pachamama rather than myself, my dreams are realized. What I need comes easily to me because Pachamama moves freely through me.

When I communicate in and through my dreams, I perceive the world through the soul of Pachamama. I overlap my story with her creation story. The goal is to have one dream—one story—written in identical handwriting. Pachamama becomes the context through which I continue to write her creation story as well as my own personal story. To achieve my destiny is to fulfill my dreams, to live with integrity, to be whole and holy. To achieve my destiny is to live in communion with Pachamama.

Reflection:

The Achuar believe there is a dream dreaming them. Because they relate to Pachamama through the intimacy of their dreams and hearts, they have a sense of being known by her, understood by her and loved by her. All people, those in the South and those in the North, are part of this dream; part of this vision.

If there is a dream dreaming me, it is Pachamama's vision of me. She is doing the dreaming. And if I have a sense of being part of that dream, it is my heart's vision of her. I am doing the dreaming. My seeing Pachamama, then, is really my awareness of her seeing me.

- I no longer see myself as attempting to control nature. I recognize my place in the world.
- I partner with the wide scope of goodness, wherever it appears.
- I commit to preserving, sustaining and sharing the gifts of creation.
- I am one more link in a collective rise of consciousness that benefits all creation.
- I recognize that the universe and life on Earth, including me, are in a continuous state of transformation.
- I know that I am a thinking, loving being.
- I have the wisdom and courage to shift my mode of consciousness, to wake up to a new dream for creation.
- I have a sense of being known by God, understood by God, loved by God.
- I look to fulfill Pachamama's dreams as her dreams, too, look to fulfill me.
- I know where and how to find Arutum, godly energy that allows me to perform miracles in her name.

Closing Prayer:

Pachamama, I ask: How can I immerse myself in you? You tell me: I must listen to and with my heart. My heart knows all things because it comes from you and will one day return to you. My heart has held the plan for my destiny for all eternity. The more I fulfill my destiny, the more I fulfill your dream for the world.

Pachamama, you tell me no heart suffers when it searches for its dream, that is, its destiny, because every second of the search is an encounter with you and eternity. I discover new things along the way I would never have seen had I not taken risks on your behalf.

You tell me to:

Quiet myself.

Listen.

Breathe slowly and deeply.

Sleep soundly.

Dream and remember my dreams.

Pachamama, when I awake from my dreams, I feel my heart beating in synchronicity with yours. I know contentment and peace. I see things in fresh new ways.

Thank you for dreaming me into being. In doing so, I am certain you know me, understand me and love me. As I lean into you and creation in the presence of hope, I have the wisdom, courage and grace to leave this world a better place by day's end and by life's end.

I seek wisdom to these questions:

- What is Pachamama's dream for herself? What is her dream for me?
- What dreams do I have that I want Pachamama to help me fulfill? How will my life change once my dreams are met? Am I ready for these changes?
- The Achuar and Pachamama are in continuous conversation with each other. As I listen, what thoughts and words are exchanged between them?

- How can I participate in the conversation?

- The Achuar go for hours consumed by the stillness of nature. They do not need words to communicate with Pachamama or with each other. How is this possible? How can this be possible for me?

- What would it take for me to embrace the dream—the destiny—that Pachamama has for me?

- What can I do to encourage peaceful dreams? How can I remember these dreams when I awake?

Nothing is more beautiful than the loveliness of the forest before sunrise.

~ George Washington Carver

A single leaf in the rainforest represents a moment in time that Pachamama took millions of years to create. You do not have to understand the totality of the rainforest. All you have to do is recognize the completeness of one simple leaf and you will see in it all the marvels of creation.

~ Anonymous

6. Fostering My Shamanic (Healing) Presence

Opening Prayer:

Pachamama, I deeply appreciate the vast services you perform for me: the water you clean and retain, the food you supply, the soil you enrich, the carbon you entrap, the oxygen you emit, the flora and fauna you conserve and the people you shelter and protect.

Introduction:

To the Achuar, the rainforest embodies everything in the natural world. Everything in nature, all things living, natural and supernatural, are connected and working together to create a balanced and sustainable planet. All things are living and are interwoven into the very fabric of creation.

My shamanic presence enables me to experience spiritual unity with all things and all other beings. I know intuitively that humans and all life are of the same origin and creation. We are all kin.

Reflection: Give me your sacred shamanic presence.

As I embrace my shamanic presence, I shift from intellectual dominance to spiritual mutuality. It is a shift from head to heart; from abundance to sufficiency; from consumption to preservation; from dominance to interdependence; from *me* to *we*. I celebrate Earth's limited abundance from a spirit of shared sustenance.

As Pachamama calls me to steward Earth, she empowers me to act responsibly in caring for all creation. I choose to foster a shamanic presence within me by establishing mutually respectful human-earth-cosmic relationships. I seek Arutum, the energy of life, to become whole and holy.

Pachamama, like the shamans, I travel into the rainforest and the far ends of the cosmos, and return with Arutum to change human consciousness toward planet Earth. Give me your sacred shamanic presence.

- I speak and understand the language of complex creatures and simple life forms on Earth. Give me your sacred shamanic presence.

- I know plants, trees, animals and people breathe with each other. Give me your sacred shamanic presence.

- I understand humans must moderate their consumption so other life forms may flourish. Give me your sacred shamanic presence.

- I understand history must be made not within or between nations, but between humans and Earth, between people and all living things. Give me your sacred shamanic presence.

- I view nature as the dwelling place of Pachamama; the sacrament of her presence; the bearer of her promise; the center of her compassion. Give me your sacred shamanic presence.

- I realize Pachamama made the world by empowering the world to make itself. Give me your sacred shamanic presence.

- I realize Pachamama dwells in solidarity with every human being that exists, especially those who suffer disproportionately from environmental impoverishment. Give me your sacred shamanic presence.

- I recognize nature allows individuals and entire species to die, so other individuals and species may be birthed into existence. Give me your sacred shamanic presence.

- I see the dynamic power of Pachamama at the heart of the natural world and its ongoing evolution. Give me your sacred shamanic presence.

Closing Prayer:

Thank you, Pachamama, for your sacred shamanic presence. Thank you for the power of Arutum, which fosters appropriate human-earth-cosmic relationships. Thank you for the humility and sensitivity to connect with and bring balance to your world by contributing peace, harmony and health to the planet and its people. Thank you for an awareness of the sacredness of all that is; the holy interconnectedness of all that exists. Let me be one with you and all creation.

I seek wisdom to these questions:

- How does Pachamama empower the world to make itself?

- How and why do the poor suffer disproportionately from environmental impoverishment?

- Do I recognize creation as ready to suffer, to empty, to die on one level in order to bring new life forms into being on another level? Do I recognize this as Pachamama's presence and power?

- How does Pachamama comfort me? How do I reassure her?

- How might I be transformed once I breathe in the whole of creation; once I step into my role in the evolutionary process of creation?

The mystery of the living God, utterly transcendent, is the creative power that dwells at the heart of the world, sustaining every moment of its evolution.

~ Elizabeth Johnson

Places I love come back to me like music. They hush me and heal me when I am very tired.

~ Sara Teasdale

7. Journey into Sacred Space

Opening Prayer:

Pachamama, as I journey into sacred space, I bring a divine reverence and connection to the splendor of your balanced universe so I can make holy my journey through space and time. Give new meaning to my dreams by making them synonymous with the magnificence and meaning of your creation story. Let me *shapeshift*, that is, transform myself from contemporary to mystic; from passive to active; from thinking to feeling to being.

Introduction:

Soul sickness or loss, called *susto*, happens as I lose my connection with nature—as the natural world around me disappears. It is a common condition in the modern world. *Susto* probably began when humans separated animate from inanimate, consciousness from unconsciousness. This was when the soul of our planet began to slip away and crumble.

In healing soul loss, called *soul retrieval*, shamans reimagine nature restored to wellness. They journey into the spirit world to find and return lost soul parts. Healing usually takes place at night in the forest, where the Achuar return to the land of their ancestors. Healing takes place through renewed connections and visions of the river and rainforest, including animals, snakes, insects and plants. For the Achuar, the cure for *susto* is written in the bark of the trees, in the banks of the river, in the motion of the water, in the pureness of the air, in the moonlit silence of the night. The cure for *susto* is found in nature's splendor. Unfortunately, many such places are only remnants of the majestic sites they once were.

Reflection: Pachamama, make holy my journey into sacred space.

The Achuar shamans communicate with Grandmother (ayahuasca), the plant medicine that contains the spirit or energy of various life forms. The shamans use plant medicine to shift their states of consciousness. They use chants, meditation and repetitive sounds to enhance their journey. Shamans ingest ayahuasca to see through new eyes as they heal illnesses and restore balance on the soul level. They heal by helping people change their dreams about themselves, replacing a dream of illness with one of wellness.

- Let me communicate with the consciousness of air, land, water, animals, plants and all living things, and heal any imbalances I have caused within them. Pachamama, make holy my journey into sacred space.

- Send your angels, spirit guides and power animals to serve and protect me. Pachamama, make holy my journey into sacred space.

- Send my ancestors, those I remember and have never met, to protect me from harm and guide me on my spiritual path. Pachamama, make holy my journey into sacred space.

- Remove from me all misplaced energy that manifests through sickness, pain, stress or other emotional difficulties. Pachamama, make holy my journey into sacred space.

- Connect me with the soul of every person with a past, present or future relationship with me and heal any imbalances in and between us. Pachamama, make holy my journey into sacred space.

- Show me how to change my state of consciousness, thus allowing my soul to travel freely to retrieve my ancient wisdom and lost power. Pachamama, make holy my journey into sacred space.

- Help me remember my dreams, your stories when I return to ordinary time. Pachamama, make holy my journey into sacred space.

- Let me retrieve lost pieces of my soul so I can once again be present to live life fully. Pachamama, make holy my journey into sacred space.

- Allow me to see with "new eyes" in order to make my personal story synonymous with your creation story. Pachamama, make holy my journey into sacred space.

- "Hush me and heal me" when I am tired. Pachamama, make holy my journey into sacred space.

Closing Prayer:

Thank you, Pachamama, for plants and animals, for earthly formations and cosmic places, and for the many ways they complement my life and complete my world. Thank you for my ancestors, spirit guides and power animals, and for the wisdom and protection they provide me. I realize they have much to teach me. I am grateful to them for spending time with me.

Help me, Pachamama, to find empowering ways of sharing love and affection in my relationships without giving away portions of my soul and without suggesting that others do the same.

Thank you for giving me a divine connection to your world, so I can make holy my journey on Earth. Give meaning to my personal and collective dreams by making them synonymous with the magnificence and meaning of your creation story.

I seek wisdom to these questions:

- How can I birth the mystic in me? In others? In the world?
- Am I open to ask for and receive spiritual guidance?
- How do I make holy my life's journey through space and time? How can I make my story synonymous with the creation story?
- Where and with whom does healing take place for me? How might I replace the reality of illness with an expectation of wellness?
- Do I spend time each day imagining nature restored to wellness? Can I go to this place now? Can I go to this place in my dreams?

When I stand in willingness rather than will, self does not have the last word. I recover my soul, the missing link between mind and body.

~ John S. Dunne

No one, as far as I know, can adequately define religious experience, but I do think, at times, we touch into something that attains an extraordinary dimension.

~ Elaine M. Prevallet, SL

8. Healing Earth—Healing Myself

Opening Prayer:

Pachamama, I recognize and honor your presence. Thank you for giving shamans the power to connect humans with the spiritual components of the natural world. Give me the shamanic power to see the sacredness of all creation. Give me the capacity to heal your planet as I heal myself.

Introduction:

A shaman is a person who travels voluntarily to an altered state of consciousness in order to interact with entities, energy or spirits, with the intention of serving the community. The shaman performs healing rituals to alleviate the discomfort and pain from spiritual unrest, manifested in mental, emotional or physical *dis-ease.*

I must develop a shamanic presence within me if I am to foster mutually respectful relationships between the natural world and the spirit world. I must reverence Arutum, the spiritual force or soul of life, if I am to become whole and holy.

Reflection:

The Achuar believe home is a love song carried through the day by the sun and the night by the moon, forever dancing in harmony and balance.

I am always searching for home. Home is not necessarily a connection to a particular physical place. It is wherever I am rooted on Earth. It is the ground upon which I walk. It is the place of connection in my heart. It is where I belong emotionally. Home is the place where I am at peace, where I am safe and open to whatever happens. Home is a feeling of warmth. It is a moment of truth. It changes as I change.

The more I learn about home, the more I know about myself. Home is my story forever unfolding. It is my journey forever moving forward. Home is all that feels familiar and comfortable, yet inspires me to always and forever be more.

As I walk my journey, I let my footsteps fall gently upon Pachamama. As I kneel and lay upon her, I feel our hearts beat as one. I remember how she feels, how she smells, how she speaks. I listen to her ancient songs that need no words. I see her beauty, feel her power and know her peace. I rest gently in her loving embrace, for I am home.

- Pachamama, show me the sacred dimension of reality where everything with form and substance has a spirit.
- Give me a direct connection with the spiritual dimension of the universe so my travels become sacred journeys.
- Let my soul traverse that sacred realm where I can communicate and interact with the spirits of my ancient ancestors, departed family members and friends.
- Send me spiritual teachers, in human and symbolic form, to instruct, guide and assist me.
- Give me the power to align events in ordinary reality with the greater divine harmony of the universe.
- Give me the grace to help myself and others grow spiritually in order to restore and maintain harmony on the planet.
- Give me the courage to call organizations and institutions to greater harmony and justice in the world.
- Give me the power of soul retrieval that I might assist those who are sick and suffering retrieve those parts of their identity that have been lost or stolen, causing fragmentation, illness and injury.
- Identify and send me guardian angels, spiritual guides and power animals to protect, assist and serve me and others, for it is through strong and lasting connections with these spirits that my own spirituality and development take on new dimensions.
- Give me a deep, organic relationship with you, and strong connections with your spirits of nature, that I may come to know what is holy about the world and me.
- Let me connect deeply with the sacredness of the natural world, that I may contribute to its social and ecological construction rather than destruction.
- Give me your power to interact with spirits that I will find and receive healing, wholeness and holiness for myself and the world.

Closing Prayer:

Pachamama, I ask for your shamanic presence in this modern world. Help indigenous and modern cultures come together in search of mutual resolutions to planetary problems. It is your Arutum—your Spirit—working among and through us that will restore peace and harmony to the world and its inhabitants.

I seek wisdom to these questions:

- What draws me into deeper meaning with my shamanic powers? Let me be one with that which draws me.

- What calls me to a deeper understanding of myself and my place within the creation story? Let me be one with that which calls me.

- What is particularly challenging about deepening my shamanic presence? Let me be one with that which challenges me.

- How am I connected to the spirits of the natural world? How can I deepen this connection? Let me be one with that which connects me.

To be attached to an ancient way of life is to initiate one's personal spiritual emancipation.

~ Malidoma Patrice Somé

The only question is: Does this path have a heart? If it does, then it is a good path. If it doesn't, it is of no use.

~ Carlos Castaneda

9. Connecting with Kin

Opening Prayer:

Why is it, Pachamama, that the early cultures had the greatest vision of you and the deepest relationship with you? Why is it that modern societies continue to lead savage assaults upon you with weapons of technology intended as instruments of liberation? I join my indigenous kin in recognizing your sacredness. I share their deep reverence for life and their respect for nature that sustains it. I finally understand, Pachamama. I hope it is not too late.

Pachamama, I ask that my ancient ancestors, recent predecessors and I live in the light of your love. May we take in your light and see ourselves as part of it. May your light allow us to recognize and embrace our connectedness. Help me achieve a new level of enlightenment that allows us to contribute to and integrate into the whole of creation.

Introduction:

With gratitude, I honor and seek forgiveness from the native people whom my ancestors unjustly abused when it served their greed and ambitions. Even though the Achuar do not seek an apology, I humbly ask for their forgiveness. They do, however, request that I listen to and assist them in their struggle to preserve Pachamama. It is my privilege and duty to do so.

Reflection: Pachamama, I commit to protecting the life and beauty of your planet.

When Pachamama ushered in the Big Bang with the greeting, "Let there be light," she was referring to this present moment. As I live enlightened and connected to Pachamama and her people, I extend this awareness into my future, to my next seven generations of kin as modeled by indigenous people. Native people throughout the planet, when making decisions for the common good, ask for wisdom to know the impact of their choices on the next seven generations. Elders are fully aware that the decisions they make today will have a profound impact on the needs, survival, and dignity of family members who will live a hundred and fifty years in the future.

- As I include and preserve the values and rituals of my indigenous ancestors in developing a spirituality of Earth consistent with the creation story, I commit to protecting the life and beauty of your planet.

- As I understand and appreciate the ancient techniques and rituals that call on the powers of nature for personal healing and communal growth, I commit to protecting the life and beauty of your planet.

- As I keep alive those ancient roots in a nature-based philosophy that have proven effective since the beginning of civilization, I commit to protecting the life and beauty of your planet.

- As I renew my relationship with the timeless values and principles kept alive for me by indigenous cultures, I commit to protecting the life and beauty of your planet.

- As I support the struggles of native people everywhere in recovering and maintaining their land, resources and sovereignty, I commit to protecting the life and beauty of your planet.

- As I nurture those dimensions of knowledge and perception that have become opaque to me, I commit to protecting the life and beauty of your planet.

- As I cultivate an ability to use resources without abusing them, and walk gently on Earth, I commit to protecting the life and beauty of your planet.

- As I follow the example of indigenous people who suspend their desire for selfish independence in favor of altruistic interdependence that all creation might live, I commit to protecting the life and beauty of your planet.

Closing Prayer:

Pachamama, I celebrate the shift; the radical change that is emerging in human consciousness. This transformation transcends national, cultural and religious boundaries, and creates common ground for the emergence of a single Earth community. Stretch my vision and imagination. Allow me to see that I am connected to a much larger family than I ever dreamed possible. Challenge my old ways of perceiving you. Give me new visions that include all people, all creation and the entire universe.

I seek wisdom to these questions:

- How can I support the Achuar and other indigenous people in their struggle to remain authentic?

- How can religions and faith-oriented organizations better support the beliefs, lifestyles and rituals of indigenous people?

- What would today be like if hundreds of years ago, our ancestors had social media that allowed people to create, share and exchange information and ideas?

- Had James Madison understood the need to include in the U.S. Bill of Rights the rights of nature, would we, who live generations after Madison, still be dependent upon non-renewable fossil fuels?

- How might we break the chains of technological "progress" in order to speak, decide and act intuitively for the rights and needs of nature for future generations?

- How can I make choices rooted in the belief that all life is connected and sacred?

- How can I foster a personal spirituality that connects with the ancient rituals of my ancestors?

- How can I further a nature-based philosophy and theology in my life?

Poor people suffer disproportionately from environmental impoverishment. Ravaging of people and the land on which they depend go hand in hand.

~ Elizabeth Johnson

Social love moves us to devise larger strategies to halt environmental degradation and to encourage a 'culture of care' which permeates all society.

~ Jorge Mario Bergoglio, a.k.a. Pope Francis

10. Sowing Seeds for Global Action

Opening Prayer:

Pachamama, I am grateful for the opportunity to serve; to make commitments beyond myself that transform the lives of others; to bring about changes that seem impossible. I recognize that the call to action to heal the world is issued by you. It is you who calls me to respond to and reverse injustices against you and your people; to alter the direction of my previous, unenlightened actions. I realize genuine change is not easy. I stand ready to struggle in a state of blessed unrest.

Introduction:

Each of us in the modern world shares a deep connection with the people who call the rainforest their home. We recognize that indigenous people are the natural custodians of the rainforest. This recognition must result in actions that promote the health and well being of this vital component of our global life support system. The people in the North must stand with those in the South to determine and represent our shared environmental interests.

We must support and broaden the economic position that the value of standing rainforests is priceless and the costs associated with their destruction are devastating. We must support social and economic development projects in the South. We must promote education and social awareness in the North.

Reflection: Pachamama, allow me to be fertile ground.

Jesus describes the kingdom of heaven as a mustard seed that starts very small but eventually grows into an enormous bush (Matt. 13:31-32). It will take time for my ideas to germinate and sprout roots. Eventually my ideas will spring to life and begin to grow. My sprouting ideas need to be protected and nurtured. If they are solidly grounded, they can support differing ideas to sprout as well. The status quo would like nothing more than to stop the growth of fertile ideas. It will take time for my efforts to change the landscape of mediocrity and complacency. Perhaps my reward is in knowing that I served rather than succeeded.

- Pachamama, I sow the seeds of change needed for social and environmental transformation to flourish. Allow me to be fertile ground.

- I sow the seeds of tenacity to replenish your Earth in the face of indifference. Allow me to be fertile ground.

- I sow the seeds of capacity to work for your greater good. I do not accept the position that time is too short and the situation too grave. Allow me to be fertile ground.

- I sow the seeds of determination, to include eco-justice, that is, responding to injustices against people and their environment. Allow me to be fertile ground.

- I sow the seeds of ritual, through indigenous traditions and cultures as remedies for healing your wounds. Allow me to be fertile ground.

- I sow the seeds of mutual respect and shared abundance as I work to improve the economic plight of your indigenous people, who may be limited in many opportunities, but rich in cultural heritage. Allow me to be fertile ground.

My Request to Rafael Taish, Shaman of the Wayusentsa Community

Greetings, Rafael.

I acknowledge your goodness, and I seek your forgiveness.

Many years ago my people, Dominican missionaries from the North, came to your village with selfish intentions. They ignored the richness of your culture and dismissed your values, rituals and traditions. They tried to make you like them.

Today, many people from the North abuse Pachamama while you and your people love and protect her. My people take away her soul while your people live in her embrace. My people have no right to do these things. I come to you today to ask your forgiveness. I am sorry. Please forgive me.

I want to thank you and your people for keeping the dream of Pachamama alive. Thank you for articulating and preserving the integrity of her creation story. Thank you for showing me that all life is a single entity. Thank you for showing me how to be a universal human. When Pachamama said, "Let there be light," you and your people cherished the light and kept the flame eternal. When it was time—this time—you offered enlightenment to me and my people with the request that, together, we preserve and protect Pachamama.

Many people from the North accept the responsibility of being partners with you, not because we have earned the right, but because we finally comprehend your call and, therefore, are able to respond to your request. Many of my people embrace your people and your rainforest and we commit to your vision that these entities are really one.

I acknowledge the sacredness of this moment. I recognize and honor the ancient dreams and visions of your people. I know you and your people believe "there is a dream dreaming us." Though all people on the planet are part of this dream, part of this vision, many in the North are not even aware the dream exists.

Many of my people dream with their minds. They want to know and understand things outside themselves. Your people dream with their hearts. You seek intimacy. You want to be known and understood from within. There is a difference between our dreams. To see Pachamama with your mind is to know her and understand her. But to see Pachamama with your heart is to have a sense of being known by her, being understood by her, being loved by her, being one with her. There is a dream dreaming us. It is Pachamama's dream for all her children on this planet and beyond to live in harmony and peace with her and each other. This ancient dream is Pachamama's vision of us, not our vision of her. The people of the North will share in your dream only when our visions originate in our hearts. This is ultimately what matters.

I am committed to sharing with my people the Achuar dream for Pachamama. I will tell them your story. Those from the North who can hear will stand with you and your people. Our intentions and actions will generate new understanding and unity. Our mutual respect and love will bring our people to communion.

In the name of my people, I honor you and thank you. I offer respect, gratitude and love to you, your people and Pachamama.

Closing Prayer:

Pachamama, you are my loving Mother. You are the living womb that surrounds and supports me so I may renew and rebalance myself and your world.

Thank you for the plants and animals; they are my brothers and sisters. We all belong to the same family. We all share the same ground, air and water. We rest comfortably in the knowledge that we are all kin.

Help me reconnect with all that exists. Allow me to be the fertile ground upon which the seeds of change fall and flourish. Let me rediscover the sacredness of your planet and recommit to its stewardship and preservation.

I seek wisdom to these questions:

- What can I do to respond to the request of indigenous people; to stand with and represent their environmental interests in healing Pachamama?

- How am I moving toward eco-justice, that is, standing in solidarity with all people, especially the poor, relative to nature, its rights and resources?

- How am I reshaping my relationship with Pachamama to reflect new insights concerning planetary citizenship?

We must accept the challenge to rethink and reshape our relationship with the Divine in ways that resonate with the new discoveries about creation.

~ Judy Cannato

This we know. The Earth does not belong to people. People belong to the Earth. All things are connected. Whatever befalls the Earth befalls the people of the Earth. We do not weave the web of life. We are but a mere strand in it. Whatever we do to the web, we do to ourselves.

~ Chief Seattle

11. Let Peace Permeate this Night

Opening Prayer:

Thank you, Pachamama, for the blessings you've bestowed on me, your people and your planet. Thank you for this evening's peace that allows me to reflect, relax and restore my body, mind and spirit. Thank you for your protection and vigilance, as peace permeates this night.

Introduction:

As soft rays of light descend below the trees, it is always as if for the first time. As the frogs and insects prepare their nocturnal symphony, evening beckons with an invitation to relaxation. "Today is past," it whispers. "You have tonight and all its possibilities to rest, reflect and heal."

Peace rises with the stillness of the night and the advent of the stars and their celestial companions. Before peace can permeate this night I must anchor the evening in stillness, taking nothing for granted, and be open to whatever this evening's gifts may be.

The silence of the night is filled with the breath of Pachamama. She wants to draw from me a quiet prayer that leans on the presence of peace. She requests that I seek stillness throughout the night as I reflect on my promise always to leave the world a more enhanced place by day's end.

Reflection: I thank you, Pachamama, for your gift of evening peace.

As Pachamama dims the brilliance of the sun, she offers the moon as a night light. It is time to rest. Rest allows my body, mind and spirit to heal and restore. Darkness allows the trees to exhale in completion of their breathing cycle. I, too, have the opportunity to exhale, to release the stress and tensions of the day. My breath flows in and out, in syncopation with a myriad of nocturnal sounds and vibrations.

As I lie upon Pachamama, I feel her roots; my roots. As I connect with my ancient ancestors and departed relatives, I realize I am not alone. I was given life through them. They continue to live on through me. I sense the tension of their unfinished business. As I release my stress and pain, I also release theirs. I am the link that allows them to heal, to continue into the future as we plan for generations not yet birthed.

As peace permeates this night, I realize I am part of Pachamama and she is part of me. I release the notion of separateness. As I breathe in her strength and stability, I exhale my anxieties, fears, frustrations and inadequacies. I sense her protection and vigilance. It is time to rest in the arms of the loving Mother.

- As I savor the sun as a reminder of the warmth of your love, I thank you, Pachamama, for your gift of evening peace.

- As I defy gravity to dance with the clouds in the evening sky, I thank you, Pachamama, for your gift of evening peace.

- As I quiet myself and marvel again at your gifts of creation, I thank you, Pachamama, for your gift of evening peace.

- As I take the time and opportunity to consider everything differently, to reflect in fresh new ways, I thank you, Pachamama, for your gift of evening peace.

- As I create new dreams and possibilities that allow greatness to permeate me and my world, I thank you, Pachamama, for your gift of evening peace.

- As I commit to strengthen, heal and transform your planet and its people, I thank you, Pachamama, for your gift of evening peace.

- As I connect with life from its beginning, to this moment and into the future, I thank you, Pachamama, for your gift of evening peace.

- As I touch Earth and realize I am connected to an entire lineage of blood relatives and spiritual ancestors, I thank you, Pachamama, for your gift of evening peace.

- As I accept the position as link between my blood and spiritual relatives, past, present and future, I thank you, Pachamama, for your gift of evening peace.

- As I realize I am kin with all creation, I thank you, Pachamama, for your gift of evening peace.

Closing Prayer:

I thank you, Pachamama, for this beautiful moment that I share. It is like no other.

I thank you for the gifts of today; for the opportunity to see you in fresh new ways. I cherish the hope that filled this day and the peace that permeates this night. I take nothing for granted—not the sounds of silence, the sights of splendor nor the sacred interactions between you and your people. Tonight I lean into your peaceful presence.

I commit to leaving your world a better place by day's end and life's end. May your peace permeate this night as it pierces the darkness and shoots into the cosmos as a beacon of light and love for all eternity.

I seek wisdom to these questions:

- How, when or through whom did I experience the gift of hope today? The gift of peace tonight?
- For what and whom am I thankful?
- How might my evening dreams bring new revelations regarding Pachamama and her people?
- As I lie upon Pachamama, our hearts beat as one. What do I tell her? What does she tell me?
- What are my blood ancestors and spiritual guides asking of me? How may I remain connected to them throughout the night?

The trees are the lungs outside my body.
~ Thich Nhat Hanh

If you walk in the forest and listen carefully, you can speak with God.
~ George Washington Carver

12. There is No Going Back

Opening Prayer:

Pachamama, thank you for bringing me here, to this point in time, to this place of *blessed unrest*—this tipping point. I realize there is no going back. I do not have the option of regressing into inappropriate attitudes and behaviors. I know I must step forward with courage and enlightenment to create possibilities that support and sustain you.

I have the wisdom to discern and the audacity to create a world that is environmentally sustainable, socially just and spiritually fulfilling. I have the tenacity to improve the planet and the plight of your people. I know how to contribute to your completeness and happiness. I will make your planet more peaceful, balanced and whole. I am here for you, Pachamama, as you have always been here for me.

Introduction:

The questions of how and whether I will help heal Pachamama's wounds are not scientific or technological, rather they are personal and spiritual. Why do I do what I do? Do I use my time and skills wisely? Is my life all I had hoped and expected it would be? Am I fulfilling my destiny? Have I made positive contributions to the cultural, political, economic and social fabric of my community, my country and my world? Have I contributed to the happiness and fulfillment of Pachamama? Have I made her more peaceful, healthy and balanced?

Pachamama has given me the opportunity to participate as co-author in her creation story. In return for this honor, she asks that I acknowledge the right of all other beings to participate as well.

Reflection: Pachamama, I realize there is no going back.

Pachamama, thank you for your continuous demonstration of love. How can I reciprocate? What tangible actions can I take to appreciate, heal and protect you?

Do I plant trees and ensure they survive? Do I nurture and protect those trees that have been standing for decades? Do I protect Pachamama's plants and animals as well as their habitats?

Do I heed Pachamama's call to improve life for the poor with a spirit of courage and self-reliance, or do I hold back and wait for someone else's tenacity? Do I honestly believe the power to improve the plight of the planet is within me? Do I step forward to create change in a spirit of service and volunteerism? Do I use my time, energy and resources to provide service to others, without expecting compensation, appreciation or recognition?

What part do I play in contributing to the common good, both for those who are near, as well as those in distant places? Do I include all life forms in furthering the creation story? Do I share the indigenous belief that there are no inanimate objects? Do I believe everything has a source of energy and thus contributes to us and the creation story?

- Pachamama, I am the fertile ground upon which your seeds of hope fall. I realize there is no going back.
- I have the energy needed to allow your seeds of change to flourish. I realize there is no going back.
- I have the tenacity to replenish your Earth in the face of indifference. I refuse to accept the position that time is too short, that the situation is too grave. I realize there is no going back.
- I have the strength to work and contribute to the common good. I realize there is no going back.
- I have inherited the principles, traditions and values to make a difference in healing your wounds. I realize there is no going back.
- I refrain from putting profits over principles in order to relate to those who live humbly, with mutual respect and shared abundance. I realize there is no going back.
- I can change the dream of the modern world by creating a just and sustainable human presence for all generations to come. I realize there is no going back.
- I can help create the basis for long-term economic and environmental sustainability, which is our best hope for moving towards a more equitable and just planet. I realize there is no going back.

Closing Prayer:

I am grateful, Pachamama, that you have included me in writing your creation story. I have been with you since the beginning of time. I was there at first light. I heard you acknowledge, "It is good." I breathe the same air, drink the same water and walk the same paths my ancestors did thousands of years ago. I was with them then; they are with me now.

It is my destiny to stand with my ancestors, by honoring their values and traditions as I reclaim a more authentic mode of living and being. I assume my place within the community of Earth. I recognize my niche within the web of life at this time, my time, your time.

I honor you and all creation as a singular, celebratory event. I cannot go back to where I was a week, a month or a year ago. All I have is this present moment in time and space. All I have is you, your people and your world. I rest in your loving embrace today, tomorrow and always.

I seek wisdom to these questions:

- How do I contribute to the happiness and fulfillment of Pachamama? How do I make her more peaceful, healthy and balanced?

- How am I the fertile ground upon which her seeds of hope flourish?

- How may I step into mutual respect and shared abundance to assist indigenous tribes in preserving their environmental and cultural richness?

- How do I create change in a spirit of service and volunteerism?

- How do I use my time, energy and resources to continue the story of creation?

- How do I reclaim the values and traditions of my ancestors? How can I stand with them in calling all creation to a more authentic mode of living and being?

The people of the jungle are super-humble but they are not poor, because they have everything in abundance. The fruit, water, air, oxygen are abundant. Being humble is not the same as being poor.

~ Robert Tindall

All that I do now must be done in a sacred manner and in celebration. For I am the one I have been waiting for.

~ Elders of the Hopi Nation

13. Ode to Pachamama

Opening Prayer:

Pachamama, fill my heart so I may know you, in every moment, in everything. I have the wisdom to know your thoughts and the power to accomplish your works. In your honor, I commit to weaving my personal story, my life, into the fabric of your creation story.

As I lie on your Earth, I remind myself that I am part of you and you are part of me. I release the notion of separateness. I inhale suffering, anger, fear, alienation, inadequacy and grief. I exhale your strength and stability.

I acknowledge and connect with the last seven generations of my ancestors, beginning with my parents and grandparents. I acknowledge my spiritual ancestors: angels, masters, teachers and power animals. They show me how to live in the moment, with deep-rooted wisdom, understanding and compassion.

I connect with my indigenous friends, the Achuar, and all those who live in peace with the land. I thank them for living in harmony with nature while protecting the land, vegetation, water, air and minerals.

Thank you, Pachamama, for protecting and supporting me and all those who inhabit your planet. I reciprocate by committing to your support and protection.

Introduction:

Pachamama is a living force. She took dust and rocks and created biology. She turned fish into fowl and seawater into blood.

Pachamama supported the evolution of the human species into *Homo sapiens*. As we stood up and became conscious of ourselves, we inherited intelligence, language and culture from our ancient ancestors. We must continue to evolve into *Homo spiritus*. That is, we must use our inherited wisdom and grace to bow to our roots in simplicity and love.

Reflection: Pachamama, I commit to your protection and preservation.

- As I use your natural resources, without which I would have no existence, I commit to your protection and preservation.

- As I recognize the true roots and webs of the intertwining biology of this exquisite planet, I commit to your protection and preservation.

- As understanding and compassion pulsate through me, I continue the dance that began billions of years ago with a Bang and extends to the end of time. I commit to your protection and preservation.

- As I realize that, when I nurture you, I honor my ancestors and pass the blessing on to future generations, I commit to your protection and preservation.

- As I, like plants and animals, become part of your vital forces and sacred power, I commit to your protection and preservation.

- As you recognize me as your devoted kin, I commit to your protection and preservation.

- As I recognize and respond to you as my living, loving Mother, I commit to your protection and preservation.

Closing Prayer:

Pachamama, awaken in me your purpose and destiny. Fill me with love for myself that I may respond with integrity (wholeness) on behalf of your plants, animals and landscapes. Awaken in me my true and only nature—your nature.

Your power has sustained and protected the Milky Way for hundreds of millions of years. Let this brief flicker of conscious life indicate a point in time when *Homo sapiens* evolved into *Homo spiritus*. Let human presence on the planet mark the time when people responded to one another out of intelligence and language, as well as simplicity and love.

Pachamama, I ask that you be with me here and now as I recommit to knowing, being, and becoming the highest manifestation of your creation. I thank you for your creative presence in the world. May your breath of life continue to enliven me and those I love, as well as all life on the planet and in the cosmos.

I seek wisdom to these questions:

- How do I weave my personal story into Pachamama's creation story?

- What does it mean to *"bow to my roots in simplicity and love?"* How do I do this?

- How and when does my heart beat in unison with the heart of Pachamama?

- Who are my ancestors? How do we communicate? How are we present to each other?

- How do I act with the welfare of the forthcoming seven generations in mind?

- How do I respect and integrate Pachamama into my daily life? How am I part of her Arutum—her sacred power?

Indigenous people believe that everything in the environment has a spirit and a divine purpose. To exploit anything to the point of extinction would not only cause irreparable damage to the environment that surrounds us, upon which we are dependent, but it would also disrespect the Creator.

> ~ Ina McNeil; great, great grand-
> daughter of Chief Sitting Bull

Let our lives be incense burning like a hymn to the sacred body of the Universe.

> ~ Drew Dellinger

❧

.

Epilogue

All my life I walked with a limp created by continuously shooting myself
in the foot. I attempted to disguise my hobble to resemble commitment
and passion, but nobody bought it. In the end I exhibited only frustration,
anger and rage.

All I ever wanted in life was to belong, to have a personal identity within
a loving community. I firmly believe that, within community, I can be far
more for others than I can be alone. In community, I seek to be who I am in
relation to others, while drawing on the strength of the group to effect change
within myself, them and the world.

All my life I sought membership within existing groups and systems: my
family, the convent, the Catholic Church, schools, etc. I aligned myself with
groups of people with the intention of connecting to the power within them
and perhaps within me. It never happened. Instead, I spent a lifetime fighting the servitude in which corporate power systems held me captive. I never
found what I was looking for in any group because I was never appreciated or
respected *as an individual.* In defense of others, I also didn't respect them or
myself. These systems and I were broken. We all walked with limps but only
I and a very few others knew it.

It was sixty-eight years before Sandra Morse escorted me to Ecuador's
Amazon Rainforest and introduced me to her friends, the Achuar. Was it wis-

dom or grace that led Sandra to encourage me to wait in the canoe while the rest of the group hiked on by foot?

When the *yanaotorango* (black jaguar) and I stumbled upon each other at river's edge, I had no idea the experience would be life-changing. For the Achuar, the *yanaotorango* possesses a respected spirit that purifies and renews life. When the Achuar see a black jaguar they know immediately that radical change is coming. Fortunately, in the spirit world, the jaguar triggers immediate healing; she doesn't wait for change to occur. She is also associated with death. I had no idea meeting the *yanaotorango* in the Amazon Jungle was also a prophetic warning; I soon experienced major losses delivered in brutal ways.

For the next two years, my life spun out of control. I lost my job, my income, my home, my reputation and my dream to create educational ecstasy for Mexican-American kids in South Tucson. That ravenous jaguar devoured my ego, pulverized my pride and left me broken. When I believed I could lose no more, I taunted the beast within that now came to me in dreams: "Is there anything else you can take from me? Bring it on!" And she did.

That evening I fell and shattered my femur. I tried to retract my words and bargain with the jaguar but it was too late. Drifting in and out of consciousness, "the jag" again visited and said, "Now you are totally broken, and truly free." Once again, as in the jungle, Pachamama consumed me with grace, and offered me acceptance and peace.

The intense pain I experience today is unrelated to the verbal and physical abuse I experienced as a child. My mom and I resolved that pain through mutual forgiveness decades ago. The pain I have today is unrelated to my desire to be loved and respected by my three brothers and my Adrian Dominican Sisters. While that desire exists, I anticipate its fulfillment without negative energy expended in the waiting.

I believe the pain I have in my leg is Pachamama's unresolved grief. It is the sorrow I hold for the suffering world, especially women and children. It is the struggle experienced by the poor and powerless.

While Pachamama doesn't want me to be in pain, it's not her job to free me of it. That is entirely my responsibility. In deep meditation, Pachamama allows me to suspend the pain in my body and the pain in our world. I am free to be at peace. I have learned to embrace the pain and move through it in ways that bring me relief and rest, so I may continue to be of service to Pachamama and her people. For better or worse, pain keeps me honest; it gives me compassion; it connects me with the struggles of life on the planet. For some reason, pain makes me pay attention to my purpose, that is, my destiny of service and love.

As an Adrian Dominican, I love my Sisters deeply, but Pachamama has also given me the gift of a local, heart-opening community with indigenous roots and values. This unique community resides in the hearts of its members, and accepts everyone as individuals. This community does not constrain me or ensure I comply with its rules and regulations. It is not designed for reformation, but rather for transformation and relaxation. In this community, we trust each other to abandon our defenses in order to be with each other in loving, appropriate ways. I have no need to protect myself within this group; we safeguard each other. My hope for this fledgling community is that we grow into a global network that includes a diverse group of individuals, especially my Sisters and the poor, as we serve Pachamama and her people.

In this local community I am not considered merely another old person. I am a revered elder with special privileges consisting of time to pray, study, read, write, listen, think, feel, and simply be. As an elder, I have the privilege of holding the collective wisdom of the group, while inviting our ancestors to participate in our ceremonies and rituals, since it is their collective wisdom I hold.

I know my body is slowing down. Luckily, I still have racing thoughts. I still dream of *shape-shifting* (profoundly changing) the world. As opportunities manifest themselves, I make sure to pursue them from my heart rather than my head. I insist that well-being is mutual. I encourage women to find their modern selves within the world and their indigenous selves within their culture. As this happens, we become free. We are all headed home.

For sixty-eight years I lived on the edge between my humanness and my brokenness. But in a single moment in the Amazon Jungle, Grandmother rerouted my destiny! Today I reside on the edge where my humanness meets my holiness; where my humanity encounters my divinity. I know sacredness exists on that edge, in that moment in time and space between the two. But it gets even more wondrous. As the sacredness in me is in communication and communion with the sacredness in you, it is called *miracle*. The miracle of life and the miracle of death are one in the same. I look forward to my death, when I will finally hear Pachamama whisper without words, "Welcome home, Sister Jaguar, welcome home."

I have one remaining prayer and request. For everyone I ever knew, loved or encountered in any lifetime I want to say this:

I'm sorry.

Please forgive me.

I love you.

Thank you.

Thank you, Sandra.

Thank you, Pachamama.

Glossary

Achuar Tribe—The Achuar are an Amazonian community of some 7,000 individuals living on 22,000 square miles of land along both sides of the border that separates eastern Ecuador from northern Peru. The name Achuar means "the people of the swamp palm."

At the beginning of the 1970s the Achuar were the only indigenous people of the area who had not suffered any loss of culture due to contact with the western world. The Achuar are related to the Shuar. They share the same area, many of the same customs, traditions, and also speak a similar language.

Achuar Language—The Achuar language is spoken by people of the same name living along the border of Ecuador and Peru. Achuar is closely related to Shuar. Like other languages in the region, Achuar has an SOV (subject-object-verb) order. It is spoken by people in the Achuar and Shuar tribes of Peru and Ecuador today.

Arutum—Arutum is the Achuar word for God or Spirit. It means the energy of life itself. Arutum is referred to as the soul of Pachamama. Legend has it Arutum resides in the mighty Kapok tree.

Ayahuasca Plant—Ayahuasca (pronounced *eye-a-waska*) is a medicinal tea prepared from the rigid, brown stem of the ayahuasca vine, *Banisteriopsis caapi*, usually mixed with the green leaves of the chacruna bush, *Psychotria viridis*. Chacruna contains dimethyltryptamine (DMT). Neither plant causes any significant mood-altering effects when ingested alone. They must be consumed together in order to have the desired effect. Ayahuasca is called the Spirit Vine or the Vine of the Soul (aya-

soul/dead, wasca-vine/rope). The word *huasca* is the common Kichwa term for any species of vine.

Blessed Unrest—The term blessed unrest was first used by Paul Hawken in his book by the same name. It is the state of undeniable connection and service to all life. It is the edge; the position for those who seek an environmentally sustainable, spiritually fulfilling and socially just presence on our planet.

Creation Story—The Creation Story refers to the biblical account of how the world came to be and how we humans fit into it. It is rooted in biblical revelation and traditions that began almost four thousand years ago. This story worked for us for a long time because, until recently, our world endlessly renewed itself through its seasonal changes. Whatever problems arose had little or no effect on us, our values and our actions. Similarly, we had little effect on the destiny of the world and, therefore, our own future.

Today's interpretation of the Creation Story calls for a change in our worldview that demonstrates a reverence for all of life. It calls for an end to our history of alienation from one another and the destruction of Earth. It provides a new context for connection and purpose. It offers a new orientation that provides a moral basis for action. The Creation Story calls for the beginning of a sustainable future. It fosters reciprocity among humans and reverence among humans and Earth. It calls for the emergence of a sense of planetary citizenship. It provides the foundation for positive social, political and economic change.

Eco-Justice—*Sister Jaguar's Journey* makes a distinction between social justice and eco-justice. Simply stated, social justice refers to our response to injustices against the poor by curbing the effects of poverty and racism. Eco-justice refers to our response to injustices against the poor relative to nature and the environment, such as air and water pollution, deforestation, soil loss and climate change.

Across the planet, it has long been recognized that environmental amenities and toxic waste sites are not uniformly distributed in relation to income group, class or ethnic communities. There exist increasing disparities between those who have access to clean and safe resources and those who do not. Disparities of this kind may be the result of historical circumstance, economic and trade relations, or inadequate or inappropriate governmental regulation. Whatever their source, it is clear an interdisciplinary approach is needed both to understand and ameliorate these problems.

The recent evidence of global warming, changes in the chemistry of the world's oceans, and increasing shortage of potable water should motivate us to work toward ameliorating these long-standing sources of injustice and poverty. Given the amount of time devoted to discussing class, race, and gender issues, little has actually been achieved in effecting the systemic changes required for marginalized social groups to participate on more equal terms in the public arenas of politics, economics, and education.

Guayusa Tea—Guayusa (pronounced "why-**you**-suh") is a tree of the holly genus, native to the Ecuadorian Amazon Rainforest. The leaves are boiled to produce a tea.

For the Achuar, the morning drinking of guayusa is a social ritual where community members come together to share and interpret their dreams. Achuar men also drink guayusa to sharpen their hunting instincts and call in the "Night Watchman," because it helps them stay alert and awake.

Functioning as a balanced stimulant, the Achuar say guayusa also promotes restful sleep and good dreams. It is believed to be both energizing and relaxing. Unlike coffee, it is said to be good for excessive acidity and other problems related to the stomach and liver. Guayusa contains one of the highest concentrations of caffeine in the plant kingdom.

Kapawi Ecolodge—The Kapawi Ecolodge was built in 1996 on land owned by the Achuar Organization (FINAE). The lodge, originally jointly owned by the Achuar and a private enterprise, became wholly owned by the Achuar in 2011. Profits from this project provide a means of economic support and jobs to the Achuar located in Kapawi as well as other nearby communities. Ecotourism provides the Achuar a source of income independent of outside oil, forestry and farming industries.

Kapawi Ecolodge is only accessible by bush planes operated by Acrotsentsak, the Achuar's aviation service. After an hour plane ride over the "lungs of Earth," the plane lands on a short dirt runway. An hour ride in a motorized "long boat" (canoe) takes visitors to the Kapawi Ecolodge.

Kapawi Ecolodge consists of 20 palm-thatched bungalows on stilts above a shallow lagoon. All the comforts of home are provided: spacious rooms, solar-heated showers, flush toilets, a common meeting room, and a dining area with excellent meals.

Kichwa—Kichwa is the collective term for about 11 million people comprising several ethnic groups in the central Andes of South America, all of whom speak the Kichwa language. Kichwa is the most widely spoken language of the indigenous peoples of the Americas. The Kichwa people are located in Ecuador, Peru, Bolivia, Chile, Colombia and Argentina.

Otavalo, Ecuador—Otavalo is an indigenous town in the Imbabura Province of Ecuador. It has a population of 90,000 people. The town is in a valley surrounded by the Imbabura, Cotacachi and Mojanda volcanoes. The indigenous Otavaleños are famous for weaving textiles, usually made of wool, and sold at the famous Saturday market.

Pachamama—Pachamama is a Kichwa word used by the people in the South American Andes. Pacha means time, space and universe. Pachamama means Mother Earth, Mother of Time, or Mother of the Universe. For the Achuar, Pachamama is God. In *Sister Jaguar's Journey*, Pachamama is used interchangeably with Mother Earth.

The Pachamama Alliance, Inc.—Drawing on more than fifteen years of partnership with indigenous people, TPA provides workshops and immersion trips to the Amazon to educate and inspire individuals to bring forth a thriving, just and sustainable world. TPA weaves together indigenous and modern worldviews, connects human beings with their inherent dignity and transforms human relationships with ourselves and the natural world.

TPA was created at the invitation of the Achuar. In the 1990s, facing oil development on their ancestral lands, Achuar elders decided to reach out to the modern world that threatened their very existence. They issued a call for allies who would work to "change the dream of the modern world," and transform the culture of over-consumption driving the destruction of the rainforest. TPA was created as an answer to this call.

TPA was founded in 1995 by Bill and Lynne Twist in San Francisco, CA. Pachamama Fundacion was established in Quito, Ecuador to partner in this effort. Unfortunately, the Ecuadorian government has suspended Pachamama Fundacion's operation for assisting the Achuar in their struggle to keep the mining of oil out of their territory.

Power Animals—Power animals are an essential component of shamanic (healing) practice. Shamans believe everyone has power animals or spirits which reside with them, adding to their power and protecting them from illness and negative energy, similar to guardian angels.

Power animals need not be mammals. They can be reptiles, insects or sea creatures. Domesticated animals are generally not considered power animals because they are already in service to human beings. It is more common to have a wild, untamed animal serve in the capacity of a power animal.

It is important to honor your power animals. Let them know their assistance is appreciated. Honoring them can be as simple as saying thank you, or getting photos or objects which represent them and putting these where you can see them as you go about your day.

Quito, Ecuador—Quito (pronounced **Key**-toe), is the capital of Ecuador. It is located in the Guayllabamba river basin, flanked by four volcanoes to the east and four to the west.

The population of Quito is 2,671,000 (2014). It is the second most populous city in Ecuador, after Guayaquil. In 2008, Quito was designated as the headquarters of the Union of South American Nations.

Shape shifting—Shape shifting is the transformation of a human being into another living creature. Many indigenous cultures know the art of shape shifting. Lakota Sioux warriors would shape shift into buffalo to become better hunters. Andean shamans transform into plants from the jungle to learn their healing powers. This shamanic technique, referred to as "becoming the other," enables an individual to merge with another living creature in order to achieve true unity with all things.

Shaman—The word shaman refers to all medicine men and women of indigenous cultures who heal and connect the human world with the spirit worlds. Shamans treat illnesses and ailments by mending the soul, which restores the physical body of the individual to balance and wholeness. Each Shamanic healing is tailored to the needs of the individual being healed. Western medicine seeks to find one cure that works for many. The shaman provides unique treatment, which holistically addresses what a single person needs at a specific time.

Shamanism—Shamanism is the oldest known form of spiritual practice. It is a set of tools and techniques that connect the spirit world and the physical world. Shamans communicate with the spirit of both living and (what we would call) nonliving things. Shamanism is not a religion. It is practiced by peoples of many religions, from Christianity, to Judaism, to Hinduism.

Soul—The soul is our essence. It is our vitality, our life force. It is the principle of life, feeling, thought, and action in humans. The soul is the spiritual aspect of humans, distinct from the physical aspects.

Soul Loss—Soul loss has different interpretations and descriptions depending upon the modality of healing one is engaged in and the symptoms exhibited (dissociation, energy loss, post-traumatic-stress, depression, etc.) Sometimes a person, in order to survive, engages in a denial process so the body and psyche do not have to experience the full impact of traumatic circumstances. Depending on the level of stress experienced, the soul parts can be "lost." This means the energy or essence affected by the trauma is no longer available to the individual. Sometimes the "energies" or "soul parts" return on their own over time.

Soul Retrieval—The shaman performs soul retrieval in order to return the lost soul part, thereby restoring health and normal functioning to the individual. Soul retrieval is popular today due to the renewed interest in shamanism.

Susto—Susto is soul sickness or loss caused by the disappearance of the natural world in our lives.

Yanaotorango—Yanaotorango is the Kichwa term for black jaguar. For the Achuar, the black jaguar has a powerful spirit that purifies and renews life. When the Achuar see a black jaguar they know immediately that radical change is coming. In the spirit world, the yanaotorango can trigger immediate healing within a person. Shamans have been known to shape-shift into yanaotorangos as they conduct their business in the spirit world.

About the Authors

Sister Judy Bisignano, O.P., Ed.D.
Sister Judy Bisignano is an Adrian Dominican nun. Born in Des Moines, Iowa, Sister Judy has spent most of her adult life pursuing alternative education in Tucson, Arizona. She has two master's degrees (biology and ecology) and a doctorate in educational leadership and curriculum development. She has assisted in authoring and publishing 32 books for children and adults in the areas of values education, environmental education, aerospace and astronomy.

In her trips to the rainforest, Sister Judy spends extended time writing and praying along the banks of the Pastaza and Kapawari Rivers, where she first encountered a black jaguar preying on a large white bird. Word quickly spread among the Achuar that "the Sister in Sandra's group" had seen a black jaguar. Wherever she went, the Achuar would come to meet *Sister Jaguar*, a.k.a *Hermana Otorongo*. Sister Judy is the only person from the North to have seen a black jaguar since the Pachamama Alliance began taking people to the area in 2000.

Sandra Curtis Morse
Sandra Morse and her eleven siblings were raised in Yuma, Arizona. She is a communications philosopher and has a private practice in Tucson, Arizona. She holds a Bachelor of Arts degree in philosophy and communication and

is a certified mediator. She and her husband, Michael, have three children: Sophie, Elliott and Oren.

Sandra conducts numerous group trips into the Ecuadorian rainforest for the Pachamama Alliance. Over the years, she has developed close and meaningful relationships with many Achuar in various villages. Word spreads via short-wave radio that "Sandra is here to see us. It is time to gather and celebrate."

On a recent visit, Achuar elders of the Wayusentsa and Kusutkau communities publicly thanked and honored Sandra as "one of them." They specifically asked that she work on their behalf to organize programs whereby community members from seven Achuar villages may improve their lives through education, reforestation and health programs. All proceeds from *Sister Jaguar's Journey—The Book* will be used to make this request a reality.

For more information contact:
http://sisterjaguarsjourney.com
sandritamorse11@gmail.com
judybisignano@gmail.com